HERE'S WHAT PEOPLE ARE SAYING

Eddy Gallagher goes from room to room at the hospice, offering the residents a cocktail before dinner. And, like any good bartender, he finds himself listening while pouring. What he hears changes his life. It will change yours, too. This is not a book about dying. This is a book about living.

Fr. Bill Brock

A compelling story of a hospice volunteer who discovers meaning and purpose in his own life among the terminally ill patients he serves. The author offers comfort and reassurance to the afflicted, their families and friends who might someday have to face the hospice experience.

R. J. Rademacher, M.D.

The author has taken the puzzle piece that is the spiritual part of our everyday lives and fit it nicely into place with the more obvious and accepted emotional and physical dimensions. He's made the extraordinary seem ordinary and allowed the reader to realize the potential for more awareness of self, others, and God.

Dawn Obrecht, M.D.

I love this book—it's about believing.

Judith G. Dowling, Psy.D., clinical psychologist

To Betsy:

All The Best

Edward Bear

The Cocktail Cart

Betsy – To a very special person
Ron

Edward Bear

M&J Publishing

Other Books by Edward Bear:

The Dark Night of Recovery
The Seven Deadly Needs

Acknowledgements.
For permission to use the following selections,
grateful thanks are extended:
Delacorte Press: Illusions, Richard Bach, ©1977.
Vintage Books: The Hospice Movement, Sandol
Stoddard, ©1978. Prentice Hall: Camus; critical
essays, Germaine Bree ©1962. Monarch Press:
Emily Dickinson—Poetry, ©1965,

Cover design by Sarah Edgell.
sarah@edgellworks.com

Printed in the United States of America
First trade printing: Feb. 2001
Library of Congress Card Number: 0019313

PUBLISHER'S NOTE

This is a work of fiction. Any resemblance to
persons, living or dead, events, or locales is
entirely coincidental.

To:

All the anonymous Caregivers and Hospice
workers who, with compassion
and grace, stand with us as we prepare
for the next part of the journey.

Angels, seen and unseen.

Sweet Jo, mistress of the days and the nights.

As always, the children—Tommy (wherever you
are), Tree, Cat, Monica, Laura and Steve.

Dying is a wild night and a new road.
Emily Dickinson

Help thy brother's boat across, and lo! thine own has reached the shore.
Hindu proverb

You matter because you are. You matter to the last moment of your life, and we will do all we can not only to help you die peacefully, but also to live until you die.
Dame Cicely Saunders

Here is a test to find out whether your mission on earth is finished: If you're alive, it isn't.
Richard Bach

In the midst of winter, I found within me an invincible summer.
Albert Camus

. . .For the ayde and comfort of the poore sykke, blynde and aged persons. . .whereyn they may be lodged, cherysshed and refreshed.
From a petition for a hospice by the citizens of London to Henry VIII (1538)

Out beyond the ideas of wrong-doing and right-doing there is a field. . .I'll meet you there.
Rumi

Whatever authority I have rests solely on knowing how little I know.
Socrates

CHAPTER 1

The Hospice of Saint Michael was located at 2338 Acton, a short, cul-de-sac just behind the big All American Furniture store on Mason Avenue. Before the Hospice took over the old senior residence home, there was a sign at the corner of 24th and Acton:

DEAD END

Soon after the Hospice began operation, the city was petitioned to remove the sign. Unable to effect removal due to a city ordinance requiring the information, the compromise was a sign that read:

NOT A THROUGH
STREET

CHAPTER 2

"How did it go?" said Pam.

"I got community service," said Edward. "Can you believe it? Community service for a few lousy parking tickets."

"The Sword of Justice strikes again," Pam said solemnly. He gave her a look.

"We're talking parking tickets, Pam," he said. "Par-king. Non-moving violations. Not drunk driving or driving under the influence or running over little children in the crosswalk. I don't even drink anymore, for chrissakes."

"You tell the judge?"

"What, that I don't drink anymore?"

She nodded.

"What does he care? Judge Hardy. Wasn't there a Judge Hardy in one of those old teevee sitcoms? He just sits up there and hands out fines and community service time. You know how many hours he gave me? Hours of community service?"

"...Ten?"

"A hundred," he said. "One hun-dred hours. And to top it all off, I got a two hundred dollar fine. How could I get community service *and* a fine?"

He was a slim, ruggedly handsome six footer, his hair rapidly going gray, missing the last two fingers on his left hand.

"Nobody else got that," he said, taking a seat on one of the stools next to the breakfast bar. "Nobody. And here I am, Joe Model Citizen, hardly ever in trouble a day in my life. . .only a few minor infractions that hardly count and I get community service *and* a fine. Jeez."

"You want some coffee?" she said.

"I want justice," he said.

She ran some water and put the kettle on.

"No, my love," she said. "You probably want mercy. That's what we all want. How many parking tickets did you have?"

"Oh. . ." he waved his right hand aimlessly. "Twenty some odd. Twenty-nine I think he said."

"Well, no wonder," she said.

"Whose side are you on?"

"I'm not taking sides. I'm. . .commenting."

"Totally unfair," he said. "Undemocratic. Unpatriotic. I was in Vietnam, for chrissakes."

"Good point," she said. "You should have told him. He was probably dying to know if you'd been in Vietnam. That might have influenced his decision."

He loosened his tie.

"Pamela, I am going to strangle you with this tie if you don't stop teasing me."

She poured water over the filter, let it fill the cup and brought it to him.

"Screw the judge, Mr. Gallagher," she said, kissing him on the cheek and mussing his hair.

3

"Then he had the audacity to tell me he'd put me in jail if I ever came before him again. Here I am fifty years old, and he's threatening to put me in jail. Jeez. He said I had a total disregard for the law. That's not true. Not a total disregard. Some disregard, but it's not total. Not yet. . .What's going on? I mean don't we have bona fide criminals out there we can put in jail? Real bad guys we could be pursuing instead of spending tax dollars on a mostly law abiding citizen who has a couple of parking tickets he forgot to pay. A natural mistake. Who remembers everything?"

"Twenty-nine you forgot?"

"So my memory's not great."

"Drink your coffee while I make dinner," she said. "And don't forget to breathe. In and out. In and out. You know the drill. You seem to forget to breathe when you get excited." She kissed him again and returned to the stove.

"I'm not excited for chrissakes," he said. "I'm perfectly fine. . . .Fine. Jeez."

"Where did he say you had to do your community service?"

He shook his head.

"That's the worst part. I have to do it at a hospice. God. . . .The Hospice of Saint Michael. Downtown somewhere."

"Interesting," she said.

He took a deep breath and sipped his coffee.

"Notice how I'm breathing in and out?" he said. "Everything normal. All systems go. No high blood pressure problems here."

"Good job," she said. "I love a guy who follows directions. You get any calmer, you won't even have a pulse."

"Stevie home yet?"

4

"Soccer practice," she said. "Mrs. Barbach's picking him up when she picks up Jarvis."

"Is he okay? Stevie?"

"Yes, he's okay."

"You think he likes second grade?"

"I don't think he's sure yet. Too soon to tell. But he likes school."

"Is Mrs. Barbach a good driver?"

"He's fine," she said. "He's going to stay fine. Nothing's going to happen to him." She stopped and looked at him. ". . . It's been five years since Tommy died. Five years."

"I know, I know," he said. "It's just that sometimes. . ."

"I ever tell you my Aunt Julie was there?" she said. "At Saint Michael's?"

"Aunt Julie. . .Your crazy aunt with the parakeet?"

"Yeah. They let her keep the parakeet at the hospice. Barney, she called it. Barney, the bird. She talked to it right to the end."

"What was it like?"

"Oh, she died in her sleep," said Pam. "As I remember, it was quite peaceful."

"No, I mean what was the hospice like?"

". . .It seemed nice. As a matter of fact I heard a lot of laughter. I remember thinking that it was odd---the laughter. Here are all these people dying, and you can hear people laughing. That seemed strange. But Aunt Julie liked it."

"Just what I need," said Edward. "Some lunatic asylum where the staff is giggling while the patients die. Sounds like something out of Edgar Allan Poe."

"They had a baby there," said Pam. "I remember that. They have a nursery and everything. Two cribs. Mickey Mouse wallpaper. Those mobiles with whales and birds over the cribs. I just peeked in. They won't let you go in and look. Won't even tell you what's wrong with the babies. They just say it's a baby, and everybody loves him. Or her, I guess, if it's a girl. No names. Just a baby that everybody loves."

Edward shook his head.

"God. . .Old people dying. Babies dying. You know I wasn't around when either of my parents died. I ever tell you that? And of course there was Tommy. I wasn't there when . ."

"You couldn't have known. . ." Pamela said quickly.

"Maybe. . .My sister tells me I was emotionally unavailable when I was young. Very unavailable was the way she put it. Karen, as you know, is a psychotherapist who knows about such matters. Besides, she's six years older and she gets to tell me things like that whether I want to hear them or not."

"I'm amazed you made it all those years without me," said Pam.

"Me, too," he said. "But at least I'm better now. Better than I used to be."

"Oh?"

"Well I am," he said defensively. "For one thing I communicate better. Even Karen thinks so. I talk about my feelings. You have to admit that. Not always, but at least sometimes. . .Don't I?"

"True," said Pam. "More than you used to."

". . .You know, I'm not crazy about this whole idea. This Hospice thing. But . . .Judge Hardy probably won't take no for an answer anyway, so I might as well get used to it."

"How often do you have to go?"

"Three hours a week minimum. I figure Fridays from three to six because I get off early on Fridays anyway. Early from work. That way it won't screw up our weekend."

". . .It won't be so bad. You'll see."

"And this might be a way to say goodbye to my parents," said Edward. "Since I never really did. They died during one of

6

my very unavailable periods. Karen's probably got a word for that. She's got a word for everything. Transference maybe."

"You can be there when somebody else's mother or father dies. Or maybe just someone who doesn't have anybody to be with them."

"Yeah. . .Sounds goofy, doesn't it?"

"Actually, it doesn't," she said. "It sounds very. . . touching."

"Well. . ." He manufactured a cough. "Dinner ready yet?"

"Keep breathing. I just got started."

"What are we having?" he said.

"Meatloaf, mashed potatoes and gravy."

"God, I love meatloaf. And you. I love you a lot. You know, if they were going to arrest me, they should do it for marrying someone as young and pretty as you are."

"Keep breathing," she said. "Read the newspaper. Thirty eight is not young and I'm not all that pretty."

"Guess again, Maid Pamela."

He took his tie off and stuffed it in his coat pocket.

"Would you still love me if I was a criminal?" he said.

"I thought you *were* a criminal. Or had been. Didn't you tell me that once?"

"I was a very minor criminal," he said. "Very minor. Small potatoes. Hardly worthy of the name."

"Well, what kind of criminal did you have in mind?" she said. "That I should love."

"Jeez. Does it make a difference?" he said.

". . .Might."

"I'd love you if you were a criminal," he said. "No matter what you'd done."

"Even if I was a prostitute?"

". . .Is prostitution a crime?"

"Just keep breathing," she said. "I'm warming up the meatloaf."

". . .Well, is it?"

She turned and smiled at him.

"Depends on who's doing it," she said.

CHAPTER 3

The Hospice of St. Michael was a long single-story building that housed, at capacity, thirty eight people. The administrative offices and Father Tom's office were located at the north end. Halfway to the south end, the Dining Hall and the Main Lobby were situated on opposite sides of the wide central corridor. The Nurses' station and the Family Room were clustered at the south end. Past the Family Room was a door that led out to the garden—round metal picnic tables and chairs, umbrellas to keep the sun off, bird feeders hanging from the trees; a place for afternoon tea or quiet reverie.

Ambulatory patients could sometimes be seen moving slowly down the corridor, clutching the hand rail for support, shuffling with tiny footsteps toward the garden. And, No, they didn't need any help, thank you. They were doing quite well (you should be able to see that). They didn't need a wheelchair because wheelchairs were for really sick people. Everybody knew that.

Passage from one end of the Hospice to the other took as long as twenty minutes for some of the patients. But there was really no hurry; being in control was far more important than being helped. And that control, that small bit of freedom was all many of them had left. Most had seen the previews of coming attractions. Soon enough they would be confined to a wheelchair because they could no longer walk. Eventually, even that small freedom would vanish. What lay in store was the bed, the catheter, the awfulness of not being able to do anything without help. Even the simplest things. Eating. Drinking. Sitting up in bed. Things they had always taken for granted.

And when the final days or hours arrived, the family and friends who had gathered to witness the final phase of the journey would often be standing helplessly at bedside, studying floor tiles, window shades, light fixtures, anything but the other people or the figure on the bed. The television set would be off, the messages of hope and hype silent behind the dark glass eye. Now and then a visitor, frightened by the sight of the once-familiar figure on the bed would turn it on, momentarily comforted by faces that never seemed to age, calmed by commercials seen a hundred times before. And all the while, Aunt Gertrude, often present in body only, would be drifting peacefully toward the Promised Land.

A few wished it would be over soon, then immediately felt terrible about even thinking such a thing. Time slipped into low gear for the last long uphill pull. Visitors arrived and left, some to the Smoking Room (trying to ignore the fact that Aunt Gertrude was dying of lung cancer. Or rationalizing…*Hell, Uncle Fred smokes three packs a day and he's goin' strong at ninety…*), some to the garden where the flowers were still in bloom, some to McDonald's down the street where familiar sights and sounds reassured them that life was going on just as it always had. If not forever then at least for this one day.

Mourners in attendance thought about what they would say when Aunt Gertie finally breathed her last, mentally rehearsing the final scene while they watched the barely noticeable rise and fall of the sparrow's breast. It was all so awkward; nothing seemed appropriate. Nothing at all. They could not know that Gertie had already departed for the High Ground and, though her body continued to struggle on, her spirit had already been safely delivered.

*   *   *   *   *   *   *   *   *   *   *   *   *

Mrs. Audine McKelvey, Room 102, still spunky at ninety-four, had a knack of picking the most inappropriate times to play the grand piano in the Lobby. (She had been at St. Michael's for nearly six months and thought that her very survival should merit a few extra privileges. After all, she had seen seven roommates pass on.) Strictly off limits to patients, the piano was occasionally used by volunteers to conduct an afternoon sing-along.

Gathering courage from her afternoon bourbon and orange juice toddy (*for God's sake, boy, don't be shy about the bourbon...*), she wheeled herself to the piano (she was still able to get in and out of bed by herself, though she could no longer walk), shoved the piano bench aside, located what might have been middle C on the keyboard and commenced her recital. Always the same two songs: *Memories* and *Oh, You Beautiful Doll*...Mrs. McKelvey was nearly blind and almost deaf, so the songs all had the same ringing dissonance as she pounded the keyboard with what she thought were the C, F and G chords she remembered from Mrs. Dalton's piano class in 1920.

11

Waiting in her room across the hall for just such a moment, Betty Mathews, pudgy, chemo-bald, but still ambulatory, shuffled hurriedly to the lobby in her lace dressing gown and her white bunny slippers to join in, singing something vaguely operatic as accompaniment to whatever Mrs. McKelvey was playing. It was the singing career she never had.

Then the nurses would have to come and coax them away with praise and promises. For Mrs. McKelvey another bourbon and orange juice nearly always did the trick. For Mrs. Mathews it was words of praise about her marvelous voice (*...and you never sang professionally? My, my, Mrs. Mathews, somebody certainly missed the boat with you...*) and a promise of some extra time with the Music Therapist who came once a week. She went grudgingly, usually singing Blueberry Hill as her exit song. She liked the common touch. Though she was white and had no teeth, she managed a fair imitation of Fats Domino.

Eldon, a young AIDS patient in his mid thirties, spent most of his time in the garden tending the flowers he loved so much. Everything he planted grew. Everything. It didn't make any difference whether it was supposed to be in full sun or partial sun or total shade; if Eldon planted it, it grew. Anywhere. In abundance. He wanted the garden to be his legacy, his gift to the truncated life he knew he would soon be leaving. He got his friends to buy plants; he got volunteers to buy them; even Father Tom bought a small flat of pansies for him. *Nice choice*, said Eldon. *I like pansies*, said Father Tom. *So do I*, said Eldon. Father Tom smiled and walked away. Eldon looked down at his green Kermit-the-Frog slippers and said, *See, I told you so*.

Mary Reardon, spindly as a spider, but beautiful in a stark, *film noir* way, crouched on her bed and waited for unsuspecting volunteers to pass her door.

12

You, she'd say. Such a big voice in a tiny body. If it was time for the Cocktail Cart (cocktail hour was four to six daily), she'd ask for a Bloody Mary with a celery stalk, a radish, and some parsley in a pear tree. New volunteers didn't know what to make of her. Her eyes were too big for a face that was pinched and drawn with memories of pain. *And try not to take all day*, she'd say. *I may not have all day.* She was sure there were people out to get her, coming in through the windows when no one was looking, releasing poison gas from mythical pipes in a basement that didn't exist. She made the volunteers promise to protect her. Made them swear on an old stack of magazines she had by her bed. They all did.

Mr. and Mrs. Borstein, both eighty years of age, married for sixty of those years, were sequestered together in Room 109 dying of the same disease. The Head Nurse, Mary Blanchard, found the circumstances so remarkable, she made a special trip to Records to check. Sure enough, they were both born in Sheldrake, Nebraska in 1920, married in 1940 and now were in Room 109 at St. Michael's dying of cancer. Still together.

Miss Gladys, an elderly black lady in Room 101, spent most of her time praising Jesus in a plaintive voice, her sightless eyes open, peering at visions no one else could see. *O praise Jesus, Lo'd praise Jesus...*Her roommate, Lupe Gomez, clutching her rosary, tried to ignore the voice in the next bed, moving her lips in silent devotion to the Mysteries as she recited the rosary to herself, knowing full well that Gladys would probably spend eternity in either Hell or Limbo because she didn't belong to the One, True, Catholic and Apostolic church. Though she had accepted Jesus, it was the wrong Jesus—the Protestant one.

Irma Watkins, one-time world traveler, widow of a Nobel Laureate, worried that she was becoming a burden and that people would hate her if she didn't die soon. She loved to have volunteers come and read to her from the Book of Psalms she kept at her bedside. Her other love was crossword puzzles, but even that small pleasure vanished with the advance of stage four breast cancer. Though she still knew the answers, she could no longer write them down.

George Barnett, a tall distinguished looking black man, was seldom in his room. It was rumored that he had recently been released from prison because of terminal throat cancer and had come to the Hospice to die. Nobody seemed to know for sure. The next rumor to surface was that he was the Gentleman Bandit then making the rounds Downtown, politely but firmly relieving banks of their spare cash. He was unfailingly courteous, always well dressed when he left the Hospice in the morning, but the possibility that he might actually be the Gentleman Bandit gave rise to endless speculation.

What a wonderful place to hide, said Alberta, one of the younger staff nurses. *Who'd think to look here?* Vivian scoffed at the idea, but Viv was older, less given to speculation than her younger colleague. Tony, a giant of a man at 6'4", two hundred and fifty pounds, worked mostly the late afternoon and night shifts and had more opportunity to observe the elegant Mr. Barnett. *No chance,* was Tony's opinion. *Mr. B is not the type...* Alberta said, *You think he was in prison for singin' too loud in church, Tony?... So he's done his time and come here to die. Big deal,* said Tony...Alberta countered with, *Yeah, but what a great place to hide, eh? If you were a cop would you look here? In a Hospice? I ever rob a bank, I'm comin' here...And you'll always be welcome,* Tony said sweetly. *As long as you split the money...*

Clara Muggeridge loved her Peppermint Schnapps; it was all she ever had when the Cocktail Cart came around. Her hands were so thin and delicate you could see through them. And when she stood in front of the big window in her

14

nightgown, she looked like an x-ray. The only thing she ever complained about was the food. . .*Do you really think that a grilled cheese sandwich is proper food? Or a hamburger? A dry hamburger at that. One of the reasons I have a Peppermint Schnapps in the afternoons is for my digestion. And of course Schnapps is what Frank and I drank when we first met. Apricot Schnapps. ...Aren't they supposed to have dieticians in these places? Isn't that a state law?*

Meanwhile, David Sparrowhawk in Room 112 turned off his oxygen supply and lit a cigarette. He didn't think anyone would notice, but Mr. Ambrose, stalking the hallways with his new chrome-plated walker, diligently searching for Rule Violations as was his custom, detected the offense and thumped back to the Nurses' Station as fast as he could to report the violation.

CHAPTER 4

At first, Edward was terrified. After the initial training period when he had accompanied a trained volunteer on her rounds, he couldn't make himself go into the rooms by himself. He tried, but he just couldn't. They're dying, he thought, peering nervously into each room as he walked swiftly up and down the hallway, wishing to appear busy without actually doing anything, hoping no one would notice...What if something happens when I'm in there? What if one of them dies? What would I do?...He was already beginning to count the hours left on his community service commitment. Ninety-two and counting.

His only encounter thus far had been with Cowboy Roy, a patient who spent most of the daylight hours sitting in his wheelchair on the front porch, smoking hand-rolled cigarettes directly under the No Smoking sign (nobody had the nerve to tell him he couldn't smoke there). He wore an enormous black cowboy hat, a tattered blue robe, snakeskin boots and a dark scowl. Twenty feet away was the smoking room—teevee, ashtrays, fans, everything. But Cowboy wanted none of it—he was an outside smoker. Always had been. Bugler tobacco. He stared off into the distance as if there were a horizon out there instead of the two big elm trees and the back of the furniture warehouse.

One day he asked Edward to get him a cup of coffee. Actually told him to…*Get me a cup of coffee. Black. No sugar.* Edward dutifully got the coffee and brought it to him but was so nervous he dropped it in Roy's lap when he was trying to hand it to him. Cowboy's ensuing tirade about stupid clumsy volunteers brought two nurses and the director of admissions to still the troubled waters. Edward retreated into the Hospice, appalled by what he had done.

Soon after, Mary Blanchard stopped him in the hallway.

"You be wearin' out the hallway, honey," she said. "You ought to stop in one of those rooms you been speedin' by and say hello once in awhile. We got some nice folks here and some of 'em won't be around next week. They only got a little time left. And mostly they's harmless. Matter of fact, we have never lost a volunteer due to an attack by a patient. Never…What's your name?"

"Edward," he said.

"So you're Edward," she said. "My, my…" She looked him over. "You the one spilled that coffee on old Cowboy Roy?"

"Guilty."

"Well, don't be worryin' too much about old Cowboy, honey. He barks a lot worse than he bites. It's not about you anyway. It's more about how he'd rather be ridin' a horse than steerin' that old wheelchair around. Hard on a man been active all his life. He hates it. So he yells at us once in awhile. Keeps his mind off it. Heck, we don't mind. He's really a sweet man—he just don't want anybody to know it."

". . .Oh," was all he could think of to say.

Mary Blanchard was a black lady, an imposing figure at five foot four and three hundred pounds. She had a deep rich voice and a laugh that echoed through the hallway. Mary Blanchard was a force, a person to be reckoned with.

She took his arm and walked down the hallway.

"You see, honey, you can't take none of it personal. What they say. What they do. Most of these folks be walkin' the last mile, got only a week or two, maybe a few months. Some of 'em got regrets, sadnesses, things they did, things they didn't do. They all close to what your friend Cowboy calls the Last Roundup. You ever hear him sing? Old Cowboy?"

Edward shook his head.

"Got one of them high, tenor voices don't sound like it should be comin' from a big old cowboy," she said. "He does that one about the Last Roundup. Sings it…Gonna saddle Old Paint for the last time…"

She steered him into one of the rooms.

"Mistah Hall," she said to the man in the bed by the window. "This is Edward. He's a new volunteer." She pulled him close to the bed. "He come to change the ice in your water pitcher and see if they's anything you need…"

Mister Hall turned his head on the pillow and gave him a thin smile; his right hand drifted up from the bed and offered itself in greeting. Edward took it gently; it seemed as fragile as rice paper.

"Edward can read to you, write letters, talk about sports. Matter of fact, I understand Edward himself has played some baseball, too."

Mister Hall nodded.

"That so?" he said, his voice reedy, suspicious, his face gaunt, landscaped by eighty years of hard times and high winds. "Who with?"

"The Dodgers," said Edward. "Just minor league. Bakersfield."

18

Mister Hall's forehead wrinkled; he seemed to be frowning and smiling at the same time.

"The Dodgers are horseshit," he said.

Edward smiled.

"Could be...You a ballplayer, Mr. Hall?"

"I played some. And I wasn't no horseshit Dodger Bum neither. No siree."

"Mr. Hall played in the major leagues," said Sarah.

"I'm impressed," said Edward.

"Oh...It don't amount to much no more. Not like it did."

Mr. Hall closed his eyes and seemed lost in thought for a few moments. When he opened them he looked sharply at Edward.

"I remember things," he said. "Terrible things."

"Some things not worth rememberin'," said Mary, familiar with the direction the conversation was about to take. "Them old junk things we talked about? Best forgotten."

"Memory can be..." he appeared to be searching for the right word, "...can be cruel sometimes. I done things God His own self couldn't forgive."

"Oh, I doubt that, Mr. Hall," said Mary.

"Terrible things."

Edward's mouth was so dry he could hardly swallow.

"How old are you...Mr. Dodger ballplayer?" he said to Edward.

"Fifty," said Edward.

"I'm eighty-some. They tell me I might not see another birthday. Might not be around. You think that's true?"

Edward looked at Mary who was busy studying the ceiling.

"Oh..." said Edward. He remembered that they told him not to discuss health issues with the patients. "I don't know. Maybe you should talk to your doctor. You think that'd be a good idea, Mary?"

Mary shrugged noncommittally without looking at him.

"Doctors," he snorted. "Doctors are horseshit. Pill pushers mostly. Write a pre-scription cost ten dollars a pill. Little bitty pill. Ten dollars. Don't take no Einstein to figure out what kind of deal they got goin'."

Edward fought the queasy feeling that had settled in his stomach. Mary watched him closely.

"Maybe you better go check on Mrs. Thornberg down the hall," she said. "One fourteen? She might be needin' somebody to write a letter."

"Yeah. Sure." He swallowed hard. "I'll do that. . .But I'll be back, Mister Hall. Next week. We'll talk baseball, eh? I mean if you want to."

He was already backing toward the door when Mister Hall turned his head and vomited on the pillow. Edward bumped into the chair by the other bed in his haste to get out of the room. All he heard was Mary's soothing voice...

"There, there, Mr. Hall. Don't move now. We get that cleaned up and get you some new sheets. Time we changed 'em anyway. . ."

CHAPTER 5

The first time Edward heard the voice it was ten o'clock in the evening. He had gone to his study to read until the eleven o'clock news came on. It's what he did every night.

"...*It's me*," said the voice.

He couldn't tell if the voice was masculine or feminine. Not at first. Very ordinary sounding he remembered thinking later.

Edward looked around the room, checked the radio to see if it was on, then sat quietly for a few moments, listening... Nothing. He went back to his reading.

"*It's me...*" Same voice, a little louder.

Edward closed the book, set it on the nightstand next to his chair and stood up. Though the night was hot, an icy chill crept up his spine. All he could hear was the steady hum of the attic fan pulling cool air from the basement and forcing it up through the turbine fans on the roof. He walked to the study door and opened it; voices from the television in the bedroom down the hall were the only other sounds.

"Pam?" he called.

She hit the mute button, and the sound went off.

". . .You call?"

"You hear any voices?" he said.

She leaned out the bedroom door and looked at him. She was wearing his good blue dress shirt. He always took that as a good sign.

"Voices? . .What kind of voices?"

"I just heard a voice that said, *It's me*. . .Twice. *It's me. It's me*. Like that. Was that the teevee?"

"Can you hear the teevee in there with the door closed?"

"…No. Not usually."

"I'm watching a movie," she said. "In French…Subtitles. *C'est moi, c'est moi?*"

"I don't think so."

"…You okay?"

"Yeah," he said.

"It's very hot, Mr. Gallagher."

"Love in bloom. Requires warm weather."

"My favorite flower," she said. "What're you reading?"

"Something about the Mongol hordes thundering out of the east. Or the north."

"Good?"

"Terrific…I'll be in soon."

"I'll be here…Waiting"

"Hallelujah."

"I'm wearing your shirt. Your good blue one."

"I noticed," he said. "A good omen. I'll be in soon."

"You already said that."

"If I said it twice, it must be true."

He closed the door, walked across the room and sat down in the big easy chair. The only light came from a reading lamp. He listened for a few moments, but all he could hear was the attic fan. He picked up the book and started to read.

"*. . .It's me.*" The voice again.

Edward took a deep breath.

"*. . .Is someone here?*"

"*Yes...*"

Edward could feel his heart beginning to race.

"*...Who is it?*" said Edward.

"*Sarah.*"

"*...Sarah? And you're here? In the room?*"

"*Yes.*"

"*...Why can't I see you?*"

"*Because I don't have a body,*" said Sarah.

Edward closed the book and put his hand over his heart.

"I must be asleep," he thought. "I fell asleep after dinner and this is a dream."

He put the book on the nightstand, got up quickly and walked to the door.

"Pam?" he said.

". . .Still here."

"Am I asleep?...Is this a dream we're having?"

She walked out into the hallway.

"Is what a dream?"

"This...I mean what's going on right now."

"You sure you're okay?" she said. "You look tired. Why don't you go to bed early and get a good nights sl..."

"But I'm not asleep right now?"

"No, you're not asleep. I'm not asleep. Stevie's the only one who's asleep. And the cat maybe. I haven't seen Cyclops for awhile. He may be asleep, too."

"...I must've dozed off for a second. I'll be in in a bit. Just finish out the chapter. The barbarians are at the gates."

"Aren't they always," she said.

"Is Stevie okay?"

"Yes. Stevie's fine...sleeping peacefully."

"Everything's okay, Pam…Really."

"Good," she said, but she didn't sound convinced. "Don't forget to breathe now. Nice and slow. In and out."

"I know."

He closed the door, looked quickly around the room, then walked to his chair and stood there.

"*It's me…*"

"*…Okay, okay*," he said.

"*Have a seat*," said Sarah. "*Relax.*"

Edward sat down, put his palms on his thighs and tried to breath. His legs were shaking.

"*…I'm sitting down*," he said.

"*I can see that*," she said. "*Now relax.*"

"*Sure, relax*," he said. "*Why didn't I think of that. Relax.*"

"*Take three deep breaths.*"

He took three deep breaths and tried to calm himself.

"*I don't feel very well*," said Edward.

"*Dizzy? A little sick to your stomach?*"

"*Yeah.*"

"*A normal reaction*," said Sarah. "*Take three more deep breaths.*"

He did as he was told.

"*I also think I'm very unstable. Mentally unstable.*"

"*Why would you think that?*"

"*…I mean the fact that I'm here alone and hearing voices doesn't seem altogether…normal. Rational.*"

"*You're not alone*," said Sarah. "*I'm here.*"

"*Well, I know…but actually you're just a voice. I might be imagining all this. That's not so far-fetched. At least not for me. I mean you don't have a body, right?*"

"*Not at the moment.*"

"*So…I was thinking that people who hear voices might fall into some category like…mentally unstable. Crazy even. A religious fanatic maybe. Like Joan of Arc. Didn't she hear voices?"*

"But you wouldn't consider yourself a religious fanatic?"

"No," said Edward. *"Hardly. I'm not much of a religious anything."*

"Or a crazy person."

"No, but I have had some trouble with the police. I don't know if that counts. You see I have no way of knowing if this is actually happening. This might be an acid flashback of some kind. I mean given my history of drugs and..."

"What would convince you that I'm real?" said Sarah.

Edward thought for a moment, then pointed to the book on the nightstand.

"If you could move that book from the nightstand to the desk over there, that would go a long way toward convincing me that you're..."

"Not allowed," said Sarah. *"We're only allowed to alter physical reality in minor ways—small time shifts, temperature changes, things like that. Nothing so obvious. Unless we get a special dispensation. Moving books across the room is definitely out unless authorized. It's just a cheap trick anyway. A little practice, you could do it yourself."*

"...Why am I even talking to you?"

"Why not? Nobody can hear us."

"They can't?" said Edward.

"No," said Sarah. *"Go stand in front of the mirror over there on the wall."*

Edward got to his feet and stood in front of the mirror.

"Say applesauce," said Sarah. *"Yell it if you want to."*

"...Applesauce," he said, though not too loudly.

"See? Your lips don't even move. We're doing it all telepathically."

"And nobody can hear us?" said Edward.

25

"No. And just wait till you see some of the other things."

"...Other things? You mean this is going to go on?"

"Oh, yes," said Sarah. *"We have work to do, Edward."*

"We do? What kind of work?"

"Messenger work. You know those people you see at the Hospice on Fridays?"

"Yeah."

"It's mostly for them."

"...What's mostly for them?"

"The lessons. The messages," said Sarah. *"I'm a Teacher, Edward. This is what I do. I periodically return to the earth plane to teach, to help people during the Time of Transition. What you call Death. There are actually lots of us---Teachers. You just don't recognize us. Some even have bodies. They're mechanics, plumbers, engineers, waitresses. All kinds of people. I have the most important job on Level Six. Teaching is a sacred trust."*

"What's all this have to do with me?" said Edward.

"You're a messenger, Edward. This is the Time of Transition for the people at the Hospice. They're getting ready to journey back to the Source, and you're going to help them. We're going to help them. You and me. Us. It's all very simple."

"Doesn't sound simple," said Edward.

"That's because you have a very complicated mind," said Sarah. *"And you're unusually suspicious. Even for an earthling. You probably think I have some ulterior motive in all this. Well, I hate to disappoint you, but ulterior motives don't even exist on Level Six—that's a Level One thing. Maybe a little Level Two. But I'm no stranger to your kind of thinking, Edward. I've done plenty of time on Earth. Plenty. I wasn't such a quick study myself. Same lessons over and over and over again. My present assignment is to give you some minimal private*

26

tutoring and then observe as you go around dispensing comfort and wisdom."

"And you'll be. . .watching? You'll be there watching? Here watching?"

"Oh, yes. And listening. Monitoring the process so to speak. You yourself, Edward, have lessons to learn. Don't think for a minute that your enounter with old Judge Hardy was some kind of coincidence. You probably don't even remember asking for guidance. For help. But that's what earth life is all about. You know that. You remember the thing about lessons? It's what we agreed to back in 1950."

"Fifty?" said Edward. *"I wasn't even born until '51."*

"Bingo," said Sarah. *"Think about that for awhile..."*

Edward was quiet for a moment.

"I don't get it."

"No hurry. It'll come to you."

Edward noticed a faint glow over his left shoulder as he looked in the mirror.

"Is that you?" he said. *"Over my shoulder?"*

"Could be," said Sarah.

"You're supposed to be an angel?" said Edward. *"That the deal?"*

"Technically speaking, I'm a Level Six Teacher. But if you'd rather think of me as an angel, I have no objection."

"Level Six Teacher is fine," said Edward. *"Personally, I'm not a big believer in angels."*

"That's okay," said Sarah. *"Believing's not a requirement. It helps sometimes, but it's not a requirement."*

"Well, Sarah, I hate to disappoint you, but I don't think I'm your man for this."

"Oh, you're perfect," she said. *"Very plain. Very ordinary looking. Middle aged. A few missing fingers from the hand*

grenade episode, but nothing too serious. I mean you're not six foot four with a body like Fabio. You're just right."

"*Jeez...*"

"*People would be overly suspicious if you were too handsome,*" said Sarah. "*And all that alcohol and drug abuse that comprised your younger years actually works in your favor once you clean up your act. Helps you learn a little humility. Compassion even.*"

"*So what is it I have to learn?*" said Edward. "*You said something about my lessons.*"

"*The lessons have to do with forgiveness, trust, surrender, gratitude, God. . . the usual things.*"

"*You may want to consider the fact that I have more than a few doubts about the whole God thing. Very suspicious. Washed in the Blood of the Lamb and all that. I don't really think I'll make a great messenger. . .or whatever I'm supposed to be.*"

"*Be aware,*" she said, "*that doubt is allowed in the Kingdom, Edward. Sometimes even encouraged. Very healthy. Contrary to what you may have heard, we're not looking for a flock of sheep to blunder along behind a shepherd. It's all much more interesting than that...You took your last drink how many years ago?*"

"*Almost ten years,*" said Edward.

"*Right on schedule,*" said Sarah. "*That would put you somewhere around the Dark Years in spiritual time, about the time when nothing makes sense, when doubt reigns supreme, when you're frantically trying to figure-everything-out, and when being on the Path seems like a very poor choice. Those are the years of the Fatal Phrase—What's the use? Tough times, Edward. Time to learn about patience and perseverance...Lessons. Oddly enough the whole thing is the Good News in disguise.*"

"*Some good news,*" said Edward. "*Maybe I really am dreaming.*"

Suddenly the room turned so icy cold that Edward had to hug himself to keep warm.

"*You doing that?*" said Edward.

"*It's still ninety degrees outside,*" said Sarah. "*Who do you think is doing it?*"

"*Okay, so I'm not asleep. Or dreaming. I guess I just don't get it.*"

"*Simple, Edward. You asked for guidance and here it is.*"

"*I don't remember asking for guidance.*"

"*Wasn't that you in the car last week yelling for help? Driving down the street actually yelling...Help! Help! I'm going crazy! I'm losing it! Remember?*"

Edward nodded slowly.

"*Well, when you ask for help or guidance, be sure you're securely strapped into your seat because help comes most often in the form of being of service to others. You'll find that if you're able to stop thinking about yourself and start thinking about someone else for even a little while, truly wondrous things can begin to happen. I'm sure you've heard the phrase—I may not be much but I'm all I think about.*"

"*I have.*"

"*So the cure is getting into action, Edward. Into action helping others. It's the only thing that works. Doesn't it say that in one of those books you're always reading?* There's action, action and more action...Action is the magic word. *Doesn't it say that? Life is learn-by-doing. Pain is actually a very useful motivator in some cases. And though it sometimes seems like a spiritual scorched-earth policy, it's often the only way we're able to get your attention.*"

"*I didn't expect voices,*" said Edward.

29

"Of course not," said Sarah. *"You'd probably rather have the information come in written form—perhaps a sheet of instructions*:

Dear Mr. Gallagher, this is what We want you to do today. *"All neat and tidy. Concise. Manageable. The daily instructions. No, no. You're much too literate and easily lulled by the written word, Edward. You'll just read it and say* How nice *and go about your business. That's too simple. And far too dull when you think about it. You just ask and we'll figure out the best way to deliver the goods, so to speak. You remember that thing your father used to tell you?* God helps those who help themselves?"

"Yeah."

"Well, that's not it. It's really supposed to be: God helps those who ask. For help...Very important distinction."

"But how does all this..."

"Enough, Edward," she said gently. *"If I had a physical body, I'd have a headache by now. More will be revealed. Just trust. That's all. Someone is minding the Store. Before this is over, we're going to show you what God is."*

"I'm going to see God?" said Edward.

"No. We're going to show you what-God-is...You're not yet prepared to actually see God. You're a few millenia away from that."

"But how are you going to..."

"Just trust. Everything is working out as it should. I'll be there when you need me."

Edward thought about that for a moment.

"Where were you when I spilled the coffee on Cowboy?" he said.

"Oh, Cowboy...He has his own issues," said Sarah. *"You're helping him learn a little about patience and*

forgiveness. We accelerated his program a bit because he may not have much time left."

"One more thing," said Edward. "*Why am I getting all this guidance stuff now? I mean along with the people at the Hospice. I have plenty of time left don't I? Here on earth?... Sarah?...Don't I have plenty of time left?*"

He thought he heard the faint rustle of wings, but when he strained to listen, all he could hear was the faint whir of the attic fan.

"*...Sarah?*"

He waited quietly for a moment.

"*And will you tell me about Tommy? About what happened...?*"

But there was no answer.

CHAPTER 6

Gradually, Edward began to spend more time with the patients. He was assigned by the Director of Volunteers to the Cocktail Cart, which meant that every Friday afternoon he went from room to room offering cocktails, wine or soft drinks and candy to the patients. He loaded the supplies on the wobbly cart that served as a portable bar (ice bucket and all) and pushed it down the corridor.

He listened for the sound of Sarah's voice, but it was two weeks before he heard it again, just when he had begun to convince himself that he had never heard it to begin with, and that she was indeed a product of his own disordered imagination.

Isn't it strange, Edward? she said.

He was so startled, he almost tipped the cart over. He glanced up at the ceiling, as if he expected to see her there.

I'm just a voice, remember? I'm not up in the light fixture. Where have you been? he said.

Around, she said calmly. Just because you can't hear me doesn't mean I'm not around. Sometimes I'm very close and you can't hear me because there's so much noise in your head. Even if I yell. But I'm always there. Or here. You're never alone. Ever. Try to remember that...Besides, doesn't one of your lessons have to do with patience? Didn't we discuss that at one time?

I have no recollection of ever discussing patience with you, he said. None.

The call light over Mrs. Reardon's door went on just as he passed her room. Edward stopped to see what she wanted.

"Where've you been?" said Mrs. Reardon, both arms wrapped around her knees, rocking back and forth on the bed. "I've been waiting and waiting. You're late."

Edward looked at his watch.

"What time am I supposed to be here?"

"Four," she said.

"I'm only five minutes late."

"Late's late," she said. "I don't have all day. Maybe not even five goddam minutes."

"Sorry."

Don't you find all this strange, Edward?

All what?

This, said Sarah. The fact that you, finally into some kind of recovery after all those years of drinking and taking those dreadful pills, you of all people are now serving drinks to the terminally ill. Doesn't that strike you as. . .ironic? Funny even?

I don't know about funny, said Edward. But sometimes I wonder why I'm. . .

33

. . .First of all, it's a lesson. Everything's a lesson. You have to consider, Edward, that you have, if you'll pardon the expression, a somewhat limited view of reality. Not your fault, really, but there's only so much you can see from Level One. And maybe the Lesson Master and Her helpers are the only ones who know for sure why the lessons come as they do.

That's God? said Edward. The Lesson Master?

The God Thing is one of the advanced courses, Edward. I'm *still taking some of those. You're doing the very basic stuff—Why Forgiveness Is Important, Giving Up The Need To Know, Gratitude 101. . .things like that.*

But why. . .?

. . .The lessons come the way they come because that's the Best Way. We have people who do nothing but decide on the Best Way for each soul. Some of our very brightest people, by the way. Very important job. Next to teaching, of course. Now this lesson could be about something you'll need to know later in life, or it could mean that you're getting ready to leave the earth plane soon, or possibly. . .

You're very. . .cavalier about the possibility of my leaving.

It's not a big deal, Edward. As you well know, sooner or later, everybody leaves. I've left more times than I care to remember. It's easier than you think. Actually, being born is a lot more traumatic.

Maybe. . .But the fact is, I'm not at all sure I'm ready to leave yet. I mean I have a wife and a son. A cat. . .This may not be paradise, but it's all I've got going at the moment.

Believe me, it's. . .

Mrs. Reardon patted the bed next to her. Edward approached and sat carefully on the edge.

"I won't bite, Mr. Bartender," she said.

He laughed nervously.

34

She looked around the room before she spoke.

"I want you to know that I was never a prostitute," she said quietly. "Never. I know the stories that are going around about me, but I was never, ever a prostitute...You believe me?"

"Of course," he said.

"Really?"

"Sure. Why wouldn't I?"

Her eyes were luminous, big as moons. Her face still held the structure of forgotten beauty: the high cheekbones, the delicate chin, the finely drawn mouth.

"They're coming in through the windows at night," she said. "They attack me. You should know what they do. You especially. You've got to stop them."

"...Who's coming in the windows, Mrs. Reardon?"

"*They* are," she said. "Don't play like you don't know. And they're releasing poison gas in the basement again. Through the pipes. I told you about that last week. Wasn't it last week?"

There was no basement at the Hospice, a fact that Mrs. Reardon had been informed of many times.

"We put guards in the basement," said Edward. "Armed guards. Just last night. Marines."

"God," she said. "Marines. I have an ex-husband who was a Marine. Scared of his own shadow. Don't tell me about the Marines."

"...Marines and Army Rangers."

"Huh...We'll see."

Mrs. Reardon's name was prominently displayed on the message board in the Nurses' Station with the words **ESCAPE RISK** in bold letters. She could get out of bed and into the wheelchair by herself without too much effort. But she had trouble unhooking her oxygen tube from the large bedside tank and reattaching it to the small portable tank, and she knew she

35

wouldn't get far without her oxygen supply. She was so weak that wheelchair progress was extremely slow, a combination of pushing with her feet and trying to turn the wheels with her hands. On the best of days it took her fifteen minutes to travel between Room 111 and the front door. On bad days a good deal longer. Someone would always wander by before she made it.

"Mrs. Reardon. How nice to see you. Out for a morning stroll? Do you want to go to the Garden?"

She scowled without looking up, folded her hands in her lap and just sat there.

"The Garden, is it? Well, it's certainly a beautful day for a visit to the Garden."

She hated it that they were all so cheerful. Just hated it. She fully expected someone to stop by someday and say, *It's a wonderful day in the neighborhood, isn't it, Mrs. Reardon?* God, they were irritating.

...So do you guys up there on...Level Six is it...do you guys know when it's actually time for people to leave? Leave the earth plane?

No. I used to think that it must be written down somewhere, a big chalk board with names and dates and all that. But actually you have some say in everything that happens. Everything. Even the time of departure. You're the symphony and, to some extent, the conductor, too.

...What does that mean?

Basically, it means that life works from the inside out, not the other way around. It's an inside job. You live it and create it at the same time...Think movies.

You mean I could decide to stay here forever? said Edward. Here on earth?

Let's just stay with the beginning courses for now. It can get very complicated unless we do all the groundwork first. Later you'll understand a lot more about it.

Mrs. Reardon put her hand on his arm.

"I've decided to have the operation myself," she said. "Front and back. The whole thing." She touched herself delicately. "That way no one else will have to have it."

"...Oh?"

"Yes."

She lowered her voice to a whisper.

"I need you to help me escape," she said. "Before they get me."

"Oh, we won't let them get you, Mrs. Reardon."

"Already too late," she said. "That's why I'm having the operation. Besides, you won't be able to stop them. You won't have a chance. They'll start the poison gas, then zap, they'll get me. Eventually they'll get all of us...You've got to help."

"Trust me, Mrs. Reardon, you'll be safe here."

"They'll come when you're gone. That's what they always do. They wait outside the window then zap, they come when you leave...If you help me escape, I'll give you anything you want...Anything."

"There's no need to..."

She leaned forward and lowered her voice even more.

"You want some...sex?" she said. "I can do that, you know."

Edward looked up at the ceiling.

Silence. . . .

"...I don't think that's necessary," said Edward. "We'll make sure you're safe right where you are."

"You don't want any?" she said, raising her eyebrows. "Any sex? I'm not pretty enough? Not. . ."

37

"Oh, no," he stammered. "It's not that. It's just that I. . ."

"We could do it in the bathroom. Won't take long. And I'm good. Really good. You'll see...Ask my father."

She closed her eyes for a moment.

"...Ask-my-father," she said. "My God." She put her hand over her mouth. "You know, I was pretty when I was young. I was a looker, my father used to say. All the boys were after me. All of them. . ."

"Mrs. Reardon, you don't have to. . ."

Hush, said Sarah. She needs to tell somebody.

"I. . ." said Edward. "I didn't mean to interrupt."

She waited a moment, then took a deep breath.

"My father got there first," she said. ". . .He didn't care if it hurt. And he grunted like a pig. I can still smell him. To this very goddam day. . .I was pretty then. I had braided hair and I could run like the wind. All the boys were after me. . .Chester and Rob and Billy." She wiped the tears from her cheeks with the heels of both hands. "I'll have the operation so that no one else will have to have it." She touched herself again. "Front and back so that everyone will be safe...You think it's the right thing to do?"

He took one of her hands in both of his.

"Yes," he said. "And very courageous."

She smiled.

"You really think so?"

"I do."

"Courageous," she said. "Is that like being a Brave Little Girl?"

"Oh, much better."

". . .Good," she said. "I'd rather be courageous. My father always said that I was a Brave Little Girl. Or sometimes it was

38

a Good Little Girl. . .Did you know that Good Little Girls never tell secrets?"

"I didn't know that," said Edward.

She nodded.

"Never. Under pain of death. It makes God really angry—telling secrets. I was such a Good Little Girl." Her face was the color of ashes. "I never told anybody. . .My father died when I was twenty. Just before I married his friend, Elmer. Or was it Floyd. I remember he had hands like stone. . .It must have been Elmer because I always thought of him as Elmer Fudd. He even stuttered like that. They all died, you know."

"...Who?"

"All my husbands. I've had six husbands. Six goddam husbands. You think that's too many?"

"No...I don't think there's any set number you're supposed to have."

"It just worked out that way," she said. "They all said that I was the best, though. The very best they'd ever had...I was pretty back then, you know. And I could run like the wind."

"You're still pretty," said Edward.

"Really?"

"Oh, yes," he assured her. "Very pretty."

She touched her cheek with her free hand.

"I've lost some weight. Cancer, they tell me," she said dreamily. "I was young then. When it started. Twelve, as I recall. And pretty, too. A looker, my father always said, You're a looker, Sunshine. That's what he called me—Sunshine. I should have killed him when I had the chance."

"...Would you like me to get your drink now?" said Edward.

"What time is it?"

He checked his watch.

"Quarter after four."

39

"Then it must be time for a drink, Mr. Bartender. And put some goddam vodka in it this time, will you? Doesn't seem like anybody around here knows how to make a decent drink."

"I used to tend bar at the Zebra Room," said Edward.

She cocked her head and looked at him.

"…You sure you don't want a quickie in the bathroom?" she said. "I always pay my debts."

He released her hand and stood up to make the drink.

"Not right now," he said. "But I appreciate you asking. It isn't often a gentleman gets such a gracious offer from a lady."

She smiled and put her hands together in her lap.

. . .Not bad at all, said Sarah. You may be better at this than I thought.

God. . .Where did all that come from?

From your connection to the spirit world.

. . .I hardly think that's possible. I'm not aware that I even have a connection to. . .

Take my advice, Edward and don't think so much. It's a vastly overrated activity. Especially for you.

It's weird. . .You know I never got along with my father, either. We fought all the time. Physically fought. I actually did try to kill him. . .So, what do we do about Mrs. Reardon?

Well, said Sarah, whatever you do you'll have to hurry. I don't think she has much time left. . .She has learned a great deal in this lifetime. Hard lessons, but then some lives are like that. Now it's time she learned something about forgiveness.

But how. . .?

Oh, you'll think of something, Edward. I have nearly unlimited confidence in your ability to come up with the right lesson.

When did this go from a we deal to a me deal?

It's always been that way, said Sarah.

But I don't think I know how to. . .

That's often when you get your very best ideas—when you're not actively thinking. You think too much anyway, Edward. That much thinking is not healthy for anyone. Basically, you ask for guidance and go about your business assuming you've received it. Evidence to the contrary. I will leave you a clue, though. Go beyond thinking—it's only good for minor things.

Thinking is?

Yes. Things like eating, walking, keeping score in Pinochle games. . .Minor things.

Go beyond, eh?

Right.

Okay, I'll go beyond, whatever that means.

Good. You won't regret it.

But you won't tell me how to do it, said Edward.

Nothing to tell. You just do it.

Just do it, eh? . .Some help you are. . .

CHAPTER 7

After David Sparrowhawk had been caught smoking in his room, he was no longer allowed to keep his own cigarettes and lighter; they were to be kept at the Nurses' Station so that David would not be tempted to sneak a smoke in a building that had large oxygen tanks in nearly every room. A hand-lettered sign taped to the wall over his bed informed nurses and volunteers that David was allowed to go out to the smoking room only once every three hours for a cigarette. David didn't like the sign (which he unsuccessfully tried to reach and tear down) or any of the people who came to his room. He called Mary Blanchard Two Ton, but she gently fussed over him like he was her own.

He was a young Native American AIDS patient who had grown up near the town of Lodge Grass on the Crow Reservation in southern Montana. In the shadow of General Custard, he liked to say. The Great White Doofus.

He was especially tough on new volunteers who were unacquainted with his tactics.

"Hey, I need a smoke," he yelled at Edward as he passed the room one afternoon.

Edward dutifully entered the room, read the sign above the bed and asked what he could do.

"I need to go out for a smoke," said David.

"...Has it been three hours?"

"Four...five maybe. If I wait for you guys, I'd die from a nicotine fit. You should be checkin' in more often. See if I need anything."

David was dressed in his usual gray sweats, his upper body partially elevated in the hospital bed. His hair was jet black, uncombed, his features sharp, native, his face marked by lesions common to AIDS patients.

Edward approached the bed.

"Can you sit up?" he said.

"What's your name?"

"Edward."

"I usually can sit up, Eddy," said David, "but today I'm having an attack of something, so I'll need a little help. Here, push the wheelchair over to the bed...You new, Eddy?"

"Pretty new. Five or six weeks."

"They pay you to do this?"

". . .No."

"Then how come you do it?"

"I'm...not sure why," said Edward. He decided not to try and explain. Besides, he wasn't sure what it was that kept him coming back. He probably could have been assigned to some other form of community service. At least that's what he'd been told.

"I wouldn't do this shit for anything," said David. "They don't have enough money to pay me to do this."

Edward leaned down and swung David's feet over the side of the bed.

43

"Gloves," said David. "Don't forget the gloves. You're not allowed to touch the lepers without gloves."

You don't need gloves, said Sarah.

Edward stopped for a moment.

You don't need gloves, she repeated.

"I don't need gloves," he said.

"What if you get AIDS germs on you? What if I bite you? I might do that." He smiled for the first time and Edward noticed something he would become familiar with in the weeks that followed—David's teeth were always bloody. It gave him the bizarre appearance of someone who had recently dined on raw meat. "Then you'll have AIDS, too. I could even be a vampire."

"I'm not worried,'" said Edward.

"Why not?"

"Who's gonna take you out for a smoke if you give everybody AIDS?"

David thought for a moment, then raised his arms so that Edward could lift him and help him into the wheelchair.

"You know who General Custard was?" said David.

"Sure. The Little Bighorn."

"Right. That's near where I grew up...The Crow Reservation. Indian territory. What's left of it. You guys didn't leave us much. But then, you Palefaces prob'ly needed a lot more land than we did...Bein' white and all."

Edward eased him into the wheelchair. It was evident that David didn't like to be touched.

"My shoes," said David. "I can't go without my shoes."

44

Though he couldn't walk, David always insisted that his shoes be put on and laced up before he went to the Smoking Room. The shoes were Nike Flyers, one of his most prized possessions.

Edward knelt down, loosened the laces and slipped them onto David's feet.

"Tie 'em," said David as Edward started to get up. "I need to have 'em tied so I don't trip. I could fall down and hurt myself. Then I could sue some Palefaces. Make millions. Be one rich Indian."

Though it was apparent that David was too weak to stand, much less walk, Edward tied the laces in a bow on each shoe.

"How's that?"

David looked carefully.

"It'll do," he said.

Edward wheeled him out of his room, picked up the cigarettes and lighter at the Nurses' Station and continued down the hallway toward the Smoking Room (outside the front door at the south end of the porch, just past where Cowboy Roy sat glaring out at the world).

Nearing the Lobby, they met Eldon hurrying toward the garden in his red robe and green Kermit-the-Frog slippers.

"Planting time," he said, waving a pack of seeds. "My herb garden...Want to help, David?"

David held up his cigarettes.

"Smokin' time," he said.

"Smoking's very unhealthy," said Eldon.

"Everything's unhealthy. . .Livin's unhealthy. You here 'cuz you got a bad cold?"

"Be positive, David," said Eldon.

"I am," said David. "I'm positively dying for a smoke. How's that?"

Eldon shook his head and shuffled on down the hallway toward the garden.

David motioned for Edward to continue on to the Smoking Room.

"Guy's a faggot," he said when Eldon was out of sight.

"Oh. . .?"

"You couldn't tell?"

When they arrived at the Smoking Room, David got the lighter from Edward and lit his cigarette. He closed his eyes, inhaled deeply and tunnelled the smoke out his nose.

"You know they got a monument to Custard up by the Little Bighorn. Doofus monument. The Sioux killed him. Unkpapa Sioux. Maybe some Cheyenne. Killed the whole Seventh Cavalry, too. Why would they put up a monument to some fool like that?"

"Beats me," said Edward.

"Shoulda put up a monument to Sitting Bull...You know it was my great-grandfather killed Custard."

"Yeah?"

"Yeah...Chief Gall. That was my great-grandfather. You heard of him?"

"...No, I don't think so."

"He killed old Custard. Cut his heart out and ate it. Prob'ly tasted like shit. You'd think they'd have a monument for him. For Chief Gall."

"You know how it goes," said Edward. "The winners put up the monuments, write the history."

"We beat you guys," said David.

"...The battle, not the war."

"Yeah...The war. We lost the war. Too many white guys."

Edward nodded.

"Too many," he agreed. "We were all over the place."

"Still are," said David.

46

They sat in silence for a few moments watching a shopping spree on television. David puffed hungrily on his cigarette and lit a second before the first was half-finished.

"…You know my family's very violent," he said.

"Yeah?"

"My father beat all us kids. Beat my mother, too. She useta drink. My mother. Drink a lot. But bein' married to him…who wouldn't?"

"Your folks still alive?" said Edward.

"I shoulda protected her," said David. "Done somethin'. She couldn't help it, drinkin' like that."

"That's too bad."

"I coulda helped…" said David.

Ask him how, said Sarah.

"How?" said Edward.

"You know, she died when I was twelve. Maybe thirteen. My father beat her up a lot."

Tell him there was no way he could have helped, said Sarah. He was too young.

"You were probably too young to help," said Edward. "Too little."

"Ah, you don't know anything…"

Edward didn't reply.

"You know, my father never comes to see me," said David. "He lives just up in Niwot. Not all that far. But he never comes. He hates me…He's ashamed of me."

"Because you've got…because you're sick?"

"Yeah. And he knows that if he does come, I'll kill him. I'll find a way and I'll kill him."

47

"You think he's afraid?"

David seemed to savor the idea for a moment.

"He came to see me a long time ago," he said. "He's very . . .Indian. Long hair. Never smiles, never says anything. Just stands around and looks the part."

So what's the lesson? said Sarah.

...I need some help with this one.

Think about resentments, about learning how to forgive. Another issue has to do with acceptance—self acceptance. He can't come to terms with the fact that he has AIDS, can hardly even admit it to himself. Ask him about Bruce.

"How's Bruce doing?" said Edward.

"You think I could have another smoke?" he said. "So I won't have to come back out so soon?"

"I thought you were only supposed to have one when you came out?"

"...They never said how many. Just every three hours."

"It's one, I believe," said Edward. "And you're already on your second."

"So what's one more? We already screwed up and broke the rules."

"...Okay," said Edward. "If you tell me about Bruce."

David slowly shook another cigarette out of the pack, looked at it for a few moments, then lit it with the cigarette he was smoking.

"...Bruce was my main man," he said. "The guy I...was with. He's the guy who doesn't come around anymore. Except at night. Late at night. That's one of the nice things about this place, they let you visit anytime. So Bruce comes at night— two, three in the morning. After the bars close. Sometimes he

48

brings a friend. Frankie or Freddy or Somebody. They don't stay long. They're always in a hurry."

David tapped the ash off his cigarette.

"You know how it is," he said. "Lots to do out there. Drinkin', dancin' ...That's it, man. You know. Don't wanna spend a lot of time with somebody got AIDS, man...You wanna smoke, Eddy?"

"Don't use 'em," said Edward. "I quit."

"I should quit, too," said David. "Eldon's right. Very unhealthy. But everybody's gotta die from somethin', eh? Might as well be cigarettes. Prob'ly better than AIDS. My mouth bleeds all the time. See?" He pushed his upper lip up so that his teeth were exposed. "...You seen people die?"

"Not yet. Not actually die."

"Wonder what it's like."

". . .They say you just go to sleep."

"Who says?" said David.

"Father Tom. That's what he said during training."

"That's his job. They pay him to say that. It's all bullshit."

"...Mrs. Wentworth's dying. The Lady in 107? She's on Watch. Means she's not going to last much longer. Probably got less than twenty-four hours. She just looks like she's sleeping."

"She's prob'ly in pain."

"Doesn't look like it," said Edward. "You know Tony? Big Tony the nurse?"

"Yeah."

"He says they just mostly go to sleep. They give them enough drugs so they're not in pain."

"Then what'a you think happens?"

"...I don't know," said Edward. "I think life goes on, but I don't know how...or where."

"You suppose we get new bodies?"

49

"Maybe we don't need bodies."

"I do," said David. "This one's not worth shit anymore. I think we go to the Land of the Spirits. Where the Great Spirit lives. You believe in God?"

". . .Sometimes," said Edward.

"The best way to die is in battle. That brings honor to your family. Then you go directly to the Land of the Spirits."

"And if you don't?"

"I don't know. You get lost maybe...You heard of Ghost Dancers?"

"Yeah."

"They danced to bring back the dead. Me, I'm a good dancer. Ask anybody. I could be a Ghost Dancer. Bring back the dead...Bring back my mother."

"That'd be nice," said Edward. "Bring back your mother."

"Your mother alive?" said David.

"No...But she was a warrior."

"Oh...?"

"She and my father had a war," said Edward, trying to control his voice. "Went on for years. Then in the last battle, my mother died...You suppose she went right to the Land of the Spirits? Where the Great Spirit lives?"

David took a long drag on his cigarette and looked at the television.

"You know I'm a faggot," he said. "A Native American faggot. You ever hear of that?"

"Yeah," said Edward.

David exhaled slowly.

"That's it?" he said. ". . .Yeah?"

"There supposed to be more?"

"I don't know. Usually is...You know that's why my father doesn't come to see me."

"Because you're gay?"

"He can't deal with it. Doesn't know what to make of it, having a faggot for a son. So he just ignores me. Pretends I don't exist."

"When was the last time you saw him?" said Edward.

"Long time ago. I was living downtown, by the Mission. He came once. Wanted to take me home."

"Were you sick then?" said Edward.

"Yeah."

"You didn't want to go home?"

"...No. I belong downtown. On the street. I don't want no charity from him. Or anybody..." He rubbed his teeth with his index finger and looked at the blood. "You know there's stuff grows in my mouth, man. Fuzz. Just grows there. Like hair. Not supposed to be things growin' in your mouth. Sometimes I think it'll grow and grow and finally choke me to death. Makes me crazy...You better take me back now. I need my medication. Tell Tony I need my drugs. Tony on tonight? Or Alberta? Hope it's not her. She likes to see me suffer. Never gives me my meds on time. Always makes me wait." He shook his head. "Some fuckin' people, man. Some people."

Edward got up to wheel him back inside.

"My mouth bleeds, too," said David. "I taste blood all the time. Twenty-four hours a day, blood in my mouth. You know what blood tastes like?"

"Yeah."

"Not great, eh?"

"Not as a steady diet," said Edward.

"I'm gonna die soon, man. I can feel it. I don't want to die here. I want to go back to the reservation."

Tell him you won't let him die here, said Sarah.

. . .I don't have a clue about how to stop that from happening, said Edward.

51

Trust me, we have things in store for our Native American friend here. Just tell him you won't let it happen.

"I won't let you die here," said Edward.

David looked at him suspiciously.

"This another phony white man's Treaty for his little red brother?"

"Nope," said Edward. "I promise I won't let you die here."

. . .I hope you know what you're doing, said Edward. . . Sarah? . . Sarah? . .

I'm here. I'm here. I heard you. Relax. . .

"Man," said David, shaking his head. "...I could sure use another smoke."

"Call me in three hours," said Edward. "If I'm not in, leave a message."

"Some help you are. You'll be gone in three hours."

"That's the message," said Edward.

"Back to the room, Paleface. You guys gotta be good for something."

David was grinning as Edward turned the wheelchair around and headed back into the Hospice. His teeth were blood red.

CHAPTER 8

Every Friday afternoon at two-thirty, Mrs. Jason Everly served High Tea for the patients in the Family Room. You could set your calendar by Mrs. Everly, British expatriate, widow of the late Colonel Jason Everly who was killed while serving under General Montgomery in the Libyan desert during WWII. Neither rain nor snow nor virtually impassable roads could keep her from her appointed rounds. She brought the teapots, the tea, the china, the scones, the tarts, butter, raspberries, napkins and silverware—she left nothing to chance. Occasionally there were watercress or cucumber finger sandwiches. There was always good cheer, a smiling face and a clipped British accent. At two o'clock she sent the volunteers off to fetch the ambulatory patients and those who could be coaxed into wheelchairs. The others who wished tea were served in their rooms.

"Is the food safe?" said Mrs. Muggeridge to no one in particular, picking at a raspberry tart. "You know the hamburgers are always very dry. And the stew?" She put her fingers to the base of her throat. "My oh my…You'd think they'd have food inspectors here. Isn't that a state law?" She was as thin as a beggar.

Mrs. Everly assured her that the food was perfectly safe.

"...State inspected?" said Mrs. Muggeridge.

"Of course, dear."

Mrs. Watkins was wheeled through the door with the Book of Psalms open on her lap.

"The Twenty Third Psalm is my favorite," she said.

"Praise Jesus," said Miss Gladys, tiny as a teacup, safely tucked into a corner of the couch.

"...Yea, though I walk through the valley..." said Mrs. Watkins "the valley of the shadow of death...I shall fear no evil."

"Thy rod and Thy staff they comfits me," said Miss Gladys.

"Roger never liked any of the Psalms," said Mrs. Watkins. "My husband Roger. He didn't much like any prayers."

"Praise Jesus," said Miss Gladys, nodding vigorously into her sightless world. "He prob'ly in Hell. God love a prayerful man."

"Roger was a Nobel Prize winner. My husband. Chemistry. Lipids...or peptides, something like that. We went to Sweden to get the prize. The King was there. Can you imagine that?... King Gustave, I think."

Mr. Ambrose came thumping in with his new chrome walker, attired as always in the maroon smoking jacket he loved, and his best pair of light gray sweat pants. He considered the combination stylish. His hair, as wild and unruly as his features, resisted all efforts to tame it, though it was not for lack of trying.

"King Kong?" he said. "I remember that. Helluva movie. Mae Wray and the gorilla. I never forget a movie. Not once I seen it."

"No, no," said Mrs. Watkins. "King Gustave. The King of Sweden. Or somewhere."

Mr. Ambrose stopped for a moment, furrowed his brow and stared across the room.

"King Gustave," he said. "Don't remember it. That the one with Yul Bender? About the King?"

"What a friend we has in Jesus," said Miss Gladys.

"God save the King, ma'm," said Mr. Ambrose when he saw Mrs. Everly pouring tea.

". . .The Queen," she said without looking up.

"Her, too," he said. "I was in England during the War, ma'm. U.S. Navy."

"Were you?" she said conversationally.

"Even went out with one of your British girls. Jilly Johnson. She was from Scunthorpe or somewheres near."

"Scunthorpe," said Mrs. Everly. "Good old Scunny. I'm from Manchester. Not far away."

"Nice lady, that Jilly," he said. "A little broad in the beam, though. For a while there I almost had two wives...Ha ha ha."

Mrs. Everly didn't ask him to explain.

Mrs. Mathews donned her blond Kmart wig and entered the Family Room in her lace dressing gown humming something from Gilbert and Sullivan.

"Oh, Mrs. Mathews," said Mrs. Everly. "Happy birthday."

Mrs. Mathews looked blank.

"Happy birth-day," said Mrs. Everly.

"It's my birthday?" she said. "Really?"

"Yes."

"...How old am I?"

"Oh..." Mrs. Everly shrugged her shoulders. "What difference does it make? I brought you a little cake." She opened a small box and took out an oversize cupcake with a single candle on top. Mrs. Mathews was close to tears.

55

"I had no idea," she said, beginning to sniffle.

Mrs. Everly lit the candle and began singing Happy Birthday just as Big Tony wheeled Mrs. McKelvey in to join the off-key chorus.

"Whose birthday?" said Tony.

"Mrs. Mathews," said Mrs. Everly.

Tony took her aside.

"It's not her birthday," he said quietly. "The name on the July birthday list is Mrs. Murcheson. She's in 112."

Mrs. Everly looked crushed.

"Oh, no," she said.

"Not to worry," said Tony, gently touching her arm. "So she gets an extra birthday this time around. She has brain cancer; doesn't have any idea whether it's her birthday or not. Sometimes I think we ought to have birthdays every month. For everybody. What can it hurt? Besides, Mrs. Murcheson's in a coma. She'll never know."

"Whose birthday?" said Mrs. McKelvey. "I didn't hear."

"Mrs. Mathews," Tony said loudly.

"Oh, Mrs. Mathews,"said Mrs. McKelvey. "I see. How nice...Who's Mrs. Mathews?"

"Me," said Mrs. Mathews, still sniffling.

"How old are you, dearie?"

"I...I'm not sure." She looked at Tony.

"I believe you're just the right age," he said.

"Isn't that nice," said Mrs. McKelvey. "Being a ripe age and all. I'm ninety four."

"...Really."

Mrs. Everly lit the candle, and Tony held it for Mrs. Mathews to blow out. She took a deep breath and blew slightly to the left of the flame—the candle flickered but didn't go out.

"Oh, dear,"she said.

"Once more," said Tony.

She took two deep breaths and blew with all her might—nothing. Tony tried to move the cupcake in the direction she was blowing, but it was too late.

"…I can't do it," she said, her lower lip trembling. "My blower's gone."

"Just once more," said Tony. "For me…"

Mrs. Mathews straightened her shoulders, took another breath and exhaled just as Tony blew out the candle.

"See?" said Tony. "Third time's the charm."

"Did it go out?" she said.

"Like it was in a windstorm," said Tony.

"I…I can hardly see the candle, Tony. Or the cake. Cupcake is it? It's all very dim"

"Come and sit down," said Tony, leading her to the couch. "It'll pass. It's just the excitement."

"Praise Jesus," said Miss Gladys.

"Johnny Belinda," said Mr. Ambrose, punctuating his words by thumping his walker on the floor. "Helluva movie. About this blind lady. I remember movies. People always remark on how good my memory is. I got a memory of a person twice my age."

"Indeed," said Mrs. Everly.

"I'm not blind," said Mrs. Mathews. "…The light's just dim."

"Temporarily making do with limited vision," said Tony. "That's all."

Mrs. Reardon came through the door ever so slowly and began to make her way across the room toward the table, propelling her wheelchair with tiny steps.

"I was never a prostitute," she said. "Never. Anybody says I was is a goddam liar."

"Klute," said Mr. Ambrose. "Remember that? The movie about this hooker lady. Jane something, right?"

57

"Praise Jesus," said Miss Gladys.

Mrs. Reardon turned and glared at him with those concentration camp eyes that never blinked.

"Tea?" said Mrs. Everly sweetly.

"You got any vodka?" said Mrs. Reardon.

"No, my dear. Just tea."

"God..." she said. "Tea."

"It's my birthday," Mrs. Mathews said tearfully.

"You got any trumpets?" said Mr. Ambrose.

"...Trumpets?" said Mrs. Everly.

"Yeah. Like tea and trumpets."

"Oh," she said. "That's tea and *cru*mpets. Little cakes."

"Sure," he said. "That's what I said."

"We have scones," she said. "Nearly the same thing."

Mrs. Mathews straightened her wig and smiled through her tears.

"How do I look?" she asked Tony.

Tony kissed his fingertips.

"Like the most beautiful person in the world," he said.

"Oh, Tony," she said, dabbing at her eyes. "Really?"

"Most definitely."

"Will I be able to see better soon?"

"In a little while," he said. "A few minutes."

"Where's the kid with the cocktail cart?" said Mrs. Reardon.

"It's too early," said Mrs. McKelvey.

"Never too early for vodka," said Mrs. Reardon.

"No, I mean he doesn't get here till later."

"Catherine the Great drank vodka," said Mrs. Reardon. "For breakfast. And she did okay. Never too early for vodka."

"Or bourbon," said Mrs. McKelvey. "I love a good bourbon and orange juice in the morning."

Mrs. Reardon made a sour face.

58

"God," she said. "Bourbon and *orange* juice."

"Praise Jesus," said Miss Gladys. "I don't hold with no… a'coholic drinks and such."

"…Thou annointest my head," said Mrs. Watkins. "My cup runneth over."

"Don't I wish," said Mrs. Reardon.

Eldon came shuffling in on his worn green slippers. "The garden," he said. "Have you seen the garden?…Giant delphiniums. Hollyhocks. Sunflowers big as plates. God…"

"Beautiful, Eldon," said Mrs. Everly. "Just beautiful."

Eldon beamed.

"God made them flowers," said Miss Gladys.

"And the trees," said Mrs. McKelvey. "Remember the poem—'Only God can make a tree.'"

"How about, 'If the river was whiskey and I was a duck'?" said Mrs. Reardon. "Now there's a poem."

Mary Blanchard made her entrance, filling the doorway for a moment, moving across the room like a royal ship of state.

"Mama Blanchard here for some tea," she announced.

"It's my birthday," said Mrs. Mathews.

"That right?" said Mary. "Happy birthday."

"You think this might be my last one?" she said.

Mary Blanchard accepted the cup of tea from Mrs. Everly; it looked small and fragile in her hand.

"Truth is, you can't never tell,"she said. "Not really. Now Mrs. Criner was with us…maybe two years, Tony? Almost two. Nobody figured that long. Not her doctor. Not University Hospital. Not Medicare. No-body. So we just do it one day at a time, honey. Somebody else be makin' those decisions about which day's that last one. The Man Upstairs."

"Praise Jesus," said Miss Gladys.

59

"I have things to…accomplish," said Mrs. Mathews. "And I'm still young. Only forty…forty-eight? Isn't that what you said, Tony? Forty-eight?"

"That's very close," said Tony. "Ve-ry close. Give or take a year or two, you're very close to that."

Mrs. Mathews was sixty-seven.

"I have a career," she said. "A singing career. I mean I still have time." She passed a hand over her eyes. "I have a little…a little limited vision at the moment. It'll pass. Besides, you don't need to see all that well to be a singer."

"Helen O'Donnell," said Mr. Ambrose. "Now there was a singer. Big band. Tommy Dorset, Benny Gladman, King Stutz, all the great ones. I remember like it was last week."

"Praise Jesus," said Miss Gladys.

"Hi, Mary," said Eldon.

"How's our Master Gardener today?"

"With all due modesty, I must say that the garden is beautiful."

"And the gardener?" she said.

He deflected the question with a shrug.

"God be makin' them flowers grow," Miss Gladys said sternly. "Don't you be takin' all the credit."

"You sure these cakes are inspected?" said Mrs. Muggeridge. "They seem awfully dry. Like the hamburgers… You ever taste the hamburgers here? Criminal. Absolutely criminal. Somebody should be informed. Somebody should be in jail probably. I've lost a hundred pounds on bad hamburgers." She picked a crumb off the table and placed it on her tongue like a communion wafer.

"I baked the cakes myself," Mrs. Everly said evenly.

"Do you sing, too, Mr. Ambrose?" said Mrs. Mathews.

"I've been known to exercise my tonsils from time to time," he said, saluting smartly.

60

"Do you know 'Blueberry Hill'?" said Mrs. Mathews.

"Is that a movie?"

"No, it's a song. Fats Domino?"

"I never forget a movie. I remember once I saw a move called Shangri-la. You ever see it?"

"No...Blueberry Hill is a song. Fats Domino made it famous."

"That's a real name?" said Mr. Ambrose. "Fats? Fats Domino? A real person's name? Sounds like a pizza place."

"Yes," she said. "Rock and roll."

"Devil music," muttered Miss Gladys from the couch.

"Oh, I'm not into rock and roll," said Mr. Ambrose. "I do Big Band. Ben Miller, Ernie Kostelanitz...Like that."

"...Oh," she said.

"I'm going to my room and wait for the cocktail cart," said Mrs. Reardon, turning her wheelchair in tiny increments. "I was never much for tea anyway...though I smoked a little in my time." She put her hand over her mouth and giggled. "You know that boy that runs the cocktail cart used to tend bar at the Zebra Room. Or was it the Zanzibar? Someplace like that. And I was never, ever a prostitute. Whatever they got, they got fair and square, no questions asked and no money changed hands. Handsome is as handsome does." She began the slow, arduous journey back toward her room. She wouldn't let anyone push her wheelchair. "Don't forget to check on the poison gas, kiddies. It's still coming up from the basement. Won't be long before we're all dead...But then, nobody gives a rat's ass anyway."

"Praise Jesus," said Miss Gladys.

"And we won't have anybody to blame but ourselves when it happens," she continued. "Murdered in our beds while we sleep. Even the operation won't help then. Go-ddam..."

"Surely goodness and mercy," said Mrs. Watkins, "shall follow me all the days of my life, and I shall dwell in the house of the Lord forever."

Miss Gladys looked up and smiled.

"For-ever," she said.

"A-men, lady," said Mr. Ambrose, thumping his walker for emphasis. "Like in The Ten Commandments. Now there was a movie. Charles Loughlin and Charley Huston, I think. One helluva movie."

"Horsepucky," said Mrs. Reardon, not even halfway to the door.

"These stones are really good, ma'm," said Mr. Ambrose.

"Scones," said Mrs. Everly. "With a cee. Scones."

"That's what I said."

"Do you have a favorite psalm?" Mrs. Watkins said to Eldon.

"I'm not a very religious person," he said. "I read the comics mostly. Especially on Sunday."

"I always loved the psalms," said Mrs. Watkins. "My family were Methodists. They're very big on the psalms."

"I believe in the Great Pumpkin," said Eldon.

"...The Great Pumpkin?" said Mrs. Watkins.

"You remember the Peanuts cartoons?"

"Vaguely," she said. "Roger used to read the funnies all the time. About the little boy with the dog?"

"Right...Well, Linus and Snoopy, that's the dog, go out to their Pumpkin Patch every Halloween and wait for the Great Pumpkin to appear."

"Peter, Peter, pumpkin eater," said Mr. Ambrose, "had a wife and couldn't keep 'er..."

"Why would they do that?" said Mrs. Watkins. "Wait for the Great Pumpkin?"

"Handsome is as handsome does," said Mrs. Reardon, as she eased into the doorway. "Not a bad lesson to learn... What time is it?"

"Time for Phillip Mo-o-o-oris," said Mr. Ambrose.

"Because they believe that the Great Pumpkin appears every Halloween at the most sincere Pumpkin Patch, and they hope every year that He'll pick theirs...and they'll actually get to see the Great Pumpkin and fly off with Him as He delivers toys to all the little boys and girls in the world."

"It's a little after three," said Mrs. Everly.

"God, the time," said Mrs. Reardon. "The goddam time. Wish I was a hooker. Give me something to do till the cocktail cart came around."

"This last year," said Eldon, "Linus looked around the Pumpkin Patch and said, *I know He'll come. I don't see a sign of hypocrisy anywhere.*"

"...Did He?"

"No...But they never give up hope."

"Is the Great Pumpkin a person?" said Mrs. Watkins.

"No, He's a Pumpkin," said Eldon. "The Great Pumpkin."

"Like...Santa Claus?"

"No. Like the Great Pumpkin."

Mrs. Reardon stopped in the doorway and looked back into the Family Room.

"Only thing I know," she said, "is that a person who doesn't have anything left to sell is really poor. Really, really poor. Fortunately, I'm not poor yet."

CHAPTER 9

"You know I still get mail for Roger," said Mrs. Watkins, going through the letters Edward had delivered to her room. "Nearly a year now and it's amazing how many people think he's still alive. Even the Nobel committee thinks he's alive. Wouldn't you think they'd know better?"

"How about a little something off the cocktail cart, Mrs. Watkins?" said Edward.

She thought about it for a moment.

"No," she said. "I think not. I have to decide what to do with these letters."

"What would happen if you just threw them away?" said Edward.

"Oh, my," she said. "Just threw them away?"

"Just…tossed them out."

"Oh, I couldn't do that."

"Why not?"

"Why not?" she seemed surprised at the question. "I just couldn't. It's not the right thing to do. And Roger would certainly not approve."

Edward lifted a bottle from the cluttered surface of the cocktail cart and held it up for her to see.

"Some brandy, Mrs. Watkins? Here's a nice bottle of Christian Brothers."

"Weren't the Christian Brothers Catholic?" she said.

"I believe so," said Edward.

She sat up in bed and leaned toward Edward.

"You know, Roger hated Catholics," she said. "Hated them. He never said why. I wonder if he'd mind..."

"Probably had a mean grade school teacher," Edward suggested. "Sister Mary Margaret with a heavy ruler."

"He never said. But then he wasn't fond of religious people in general."

"Oh. . .?"

"No. Actually, he wasn't overly fond of anybody, really. I was the one who told people he was a churchgoer. Thought it might be good for his career. I...kept up appearances, made excuses, talked about his research being difficult and time consuming. He just didn't think people were very important."

Did he think she was important? said Sarah.

"Did he think you were important?"

"...Yes. Of course. What a silly question. We were married for forty-two years. But he had his research. He did some very important work, young man. Made a tremendous contribution."

"I understand he won the Nobel Prize."

"In chemistry," she said. "Nineteen sixty-eight. It was lipids, or enzymes. I never remember which. We went to Denmark. Or Sweden. We even met the King. Gustave something. Can you imagine? Irma Watkins and the King of Denmark. Wasn't Hamlet the King of Denmark at one time?"

He poured a glass of Christian Brothers Brandy and handed it to her. She took it and drank half before she set it down on the tray next to the bed.

"The King or the Prince," he said. "I never remember which one."

"Roger was always very meticulous. Very...precise. Everything had to be just so. He could be difficult. I don't deny it. And Roger would most certainly know the answer to that question...The one about Hamlet? He was very educated. Very smart."

"Tell me what it was like being married to a Nobel Prize winner," he said.

"...They still write letters to him. Did you know that? Dead nearly a year and they still write to him. To dead Roger...They aren't even addressed to Mr. and Mrs., just Roger Watkins."

Ask about the children, said Sarah.

"The children?" said Edward.

"Oh, no children. They would have interfered with his work. His research. Underfoot all the time. A distraction."

...And life before Roger? said Sarah.

"What did you do before you married Roger?" said Edward.

"I was a student. That's where I met Roger. At UCLA. I was an English major. A writer. Even had a few things published."

"Wow..."

"Oh, it wasn't so much. The old Liberty Magazine, Oak Fiction, some small literary magazines. Some poetry, too...I met him at a party. Just a chance meeting. Everyone knew he was destined for great things. Even then. He was quite a catch. We were married the day after he got his master's degree...Old dumb me, I never did manage to finish school. And even though he wanted me to work while he went to Stanford, I think he was always a little embarrassed that I didn't even have an undergraduate degree. Just two years of college and that was it."

She finished the brandy and handed the glass back to Edward. "Another?" she said.

"I'm going to make a special exception to our One Drink Rule, Mrs. Watkins and give you one more. But don't let it get around."

He added ice and more brandy and set the glass on the tray.

"Can you imagine?" she said. "I was with the King of Sweden, and I didn't even have a college degree."

"The King probably didn't either."

"Of course, no one noticed. It was all for Roger anyway."

"Do you still write?" said Edward.

"Oh, no. My. . ." As if the notion were absurd. "It's been years and years. Although—and you musn't ever repeat this—I helped him write his acceptance speech. For the Nobel prize? I helped him write it. To be truthful, I wrote all of it—the whole speech. Of course he checked it over to see if there were any errors. He made me promise not to tell anyone, but I suppose now. . ." The sentence trailed off.

"It's okay," Edward assured her. "...I bet it was a wonderful speech."

She smiled at the memory.

"Oh, it was," she said. "Wonderful. Even Roger said it was good and Roger was very hard to please. Very demanding."

Ask about the other memories, said Sarah.
Where are we going with this? said Edward.
. . .Stay tuned, said Sarah. More is about to be revealed.

"...I bet you have some good memories," said Edward.

Her smile collapsed as she reached for her drink.

"Do you think I'm too much trouble?" she said. "Too

difficult to take care of?"

"Oh, no," he said. "Why would you ever think that?"

"...I notice the nurses look at me funny sometimes. Like I'm a bother. I can't remember even the simplest things. And I'm afraid it will just get worse. What will happen when I can't take care of myself anymore? Do even the. . .the basic things."

"Then we'll take care of you," said Edward. "That's what we're here for."

"I don't understand why people would want to do that. Take care of me. I mean they hardly know me. And they didn't know Roger at all."

"It's just. . .what we do, Mrs. Watkins."

"But won't I be a bother? More trouble than I'm worth?"

"Of course not."

"That's what Roger used to say... *You're more trouble than you're worth*...Lord knows I tried, young man. He'll never know how hard I tried. Oh. . ." She seemed close to tears. "I never once mentioned to him that I knew about the women. The other women. You musn't ever repeat this either, but Roger was unfaithful to me. And not just once. He didn't think I knew. But I did. I knew. I looked the other way. That's what I did. That was the mature thing to do. His work came first. I understood that. His career. His research. He wasn't like other men. He did very important work. For mankind. For all of us. So we could have better lives."

"I'm sure he did," was all Edward could think of to say.

"Do you think I have much time left?" she said. "I mean before. . ."

"I don't think anybody knows for sure, Mrs. Watkins. Maybe you should talk to your doctor."

"I don't want to be in pain, young man. Can you tell the nurses that?"

"Of course."

"Be sure they know. I may not be able to tell them. . .later. It frightens me when I think about pain, about being in lots of pain and not being able to tell anyone."

"Are you in pain now?" said Edward.

"...Only a little. Maybe I've been lucky. It might get worse, but for now they give me drugs."

"That's good. If you have more pain, let them know and they'll give you something. That's their specialty here—pain management."

"And I don't want to become a burden. I couldn't bear it." She took another sip of brandy. ". . .Roger would know what to do in times like these. He'd give an order, snap his fingers and everyone would scurry around and get it done, whatever it was. You see, I never knew how to do things, how to...really accomplish anything. Roger said I was absolutely helpless. Of course he was right. Lord." She took another long drink. "Very good brandy, young man."

"Only the best for our guests," he said.

"...I think I'm going to die soon," she said softly. "Isn't that strange?" She squinted at Edward's name badge. "Edward, is it?"

"Yes."

"Anyway, that's what I think. I'll fall over like an old tree and that'll be it. I wonder if I'll make any noise." She sighed as she stared out the window at the birds clustered around the bird feeder. "Look at all the birds."

"Always a good sign," said Edward.

"It is?"

"Yes. The birds bring peace."

"They do? I never heard that...You know hardly anybody knows who I am anymore. I was always Roger's wife. Now Roger's gone, it's like I don't. . .I don't exist anymore. Like I never did. Even my friends, they don't. . ."

"Well, *we* certainly know who you are," said Edward.

"Miss Terranova was his secretary for a long time. She was one of the ones he...slept with. Young. Pretty. I used to call her Miss Turnover. Or Miss Informed. To myself, of course. She was the one he was with the longest. Then there was Miss Stafford, Miss Vandenberg. . .Lord knows how many more."

. . .Ask her about Henry, said Sarah.

"What do you remember about Henry?" he said.
"...Henry?"

Laduc. Henry Laduc. . .

"Henry Laduc," said Edward.
She looked at him over the rim of her glass of brandy.
"How do you know about Henry?"
"...Name just popped into my head. Weird. Henry Laduc. Like a voice—Henry Laduc."
"A voice?"
"Something like that. Maybe not a real voice that you hear with your ears, but a voice...inside my head."
"Hmmm...Henry," She rubbed the glass againt her cheek. "Henry was a...maintenance man. A handy man. He fixed things. When we lived in Palo Alto. Oddly enough, he was a young man. I always thought a handy man would be older. Gray hair, coveralls. Things like that. But Henry was young—about my age at the time."
"Interesting," said Edward.
"Oh yes, he was. A very interesting person. Not one you'd expect to find doing odd jobs. Well read. Literate...Did you know, Edward, that in the Bible, the Book of Psalms comes between the Book of Job and the Book of Proverbs?
"I'm not much of a Bible person."
"That always seemed significant," she said. "Though I don't really know why. We were raised Methodists, my two sisters and I. But I gave it up eventually—religion, everything. Well, I didn't actually give it up; I just didn't practice it much. Or at all. Roger couldn't abide religion. Or religious people.

70

Hated them. But I loved the Psalms. Still do...*Out of the depths I cry unto thee, O Lord. Hear my voice: let thine ears be attentive to the voice of my supplication*...That's De Profundis, one of my favorites. It's about pain and suffering."

"...Tell me about Henry," said Edward.

She stared out the window for a few moments.

"The birds have gone from the feeder."

"They'll be back," he said.

"How do you know?"

"They always come back."

"...Henry was the neighborhood handy man. The ironic part is that Roger was the one who introduced us. Roger brought him over to fix some plumbing—faucets or some such. They met at the barber shop. Palo Alto was a small community in those days. Everybody went to the same barber shop. And everybody knew everybody else. It was just after the war. Roger needed to have some plumbing fixed, and Henry could do that. Henry could do anything, fix anything. And Roger...Well, Roger was a scientist, a research chemist; he wasn't the fixer type, certainly not a plumber."

"Me neither," said Edward. "I'm good at the light bulb changing level, but after that I'm lost."

"...What always amazed me was how gentle Henry was. And patient. Even when the shutoff thing under the sink broke and water was coming out all over the place, he just got up casual as you please, and said, *I'd better shut off the main before we have to hoist sail.* Gentle and kind...The kindest man I ever knew."

...All the things that Roger wasn't? said Sarah.

"All the things that Roger wasn't?" said Edward.

Mrs. Watkins buried her face in her hands and started to cry.

"Oh, I'm sorry," said Edward, touching her lightly on the

71

shoulder. "I didn't mean to upset you."

"I did the right thing," she sobbed. "I know I did...I did it all for Roger's sake. Stayed with him so he could continue his research. The last thing he needed in his life was more turmoil."

Mrs. Watkins blew her nose and tried to compose herself.

"Henry and I were...together for a time. When he came over to fix things we...got together. Do you understand?"

"Yes," said Edward.

"He wanted me to leave Roger. Just. . .leave so we could get married. That's what Henry wanted, but Roger needed me and Henry was...Henry was. . ."

". . .Just a handy man," said Edward.

"God forgive me," said Mrs. Watkins. "You know what I'd do if I had to do it all over again?"

Follow your heart, said Sarah.
I knew that, said Edward.

"I bet you'd follow your heart," said Edward.

She nodded.

"I'd follow my heart," she said. "Wherever it led."

"...What happened to Henry?"

"He was killed...in Korea. He went back in the service during the Korean War. Volunteered. I'll never forget the day I read it in the paper. Pork Chop Hill. Henry Laduc. Palo Alto native. I cried until I thought my heart would break. Henry, Henry. So gentle and so kind."

"Did Roger ever know?"

"About Henry?"

Edward nodded.

"No. He was busy with his research. And Miss Terranova. I don't even know if he read the article in the paper. If he did, he never mentioned it. Nor did I."

"I'd really like to see some of your poetry," said Edward.

"Oh..." She gestured vaguely with her hand. "It's gone. Lost. I never kept any of it."

...Maybe she'd like to write some poetry now, said Sarah. What a great idea, said Edward. I know...I have lots of great ideas. Keep listening.

"But you could still write, Mrs. Watkins. You could write a poem about your life."

"My life...It's almost over. I don't know what there'd be to write about."

"I bet there's lots. There's Henry and Roger and King Gustave and Sweden and moonlight and love...Lots of things."

"Roger's dead now. Henry, too. I can't imagine anyone would care."

"I care," said Edward. "I'd like to read it."

"...You would?"

"Yeah. I've actually done some writing myself."

"Well," said Mrs. Watkins. "I'll make a deal with you, young man. You bring in some of your writing for me to read, and I'll start on a poem."

"It's a deal," said Edward. "I'll bring some in next week, and I'll expect you to be started on your poem. It could be like the Iliad. Or the Odyssey."

"Oh, I don't think my life was such an epic," she said.

"You get to be the writer," said Edward. "I get to decide if it's an epic." He got up, gave her hand a squeeze and leaned on the cocktail cart. "They're playing Bingo after dinner, Mrs. Watkins. In the Family Room."

"You know something strange?" she said.

"What?"

"I've never in my life played Bingo. I know how. And I've sat with people who played, but I've never actually played myself."

"That's because you quit going to church," he said. "That's

73

where all the Bingo players are. There and on the Indian reservations. But it's never too late to learn."

"...You think they play Bingo in heaven, Edward?"

"I imagine. There's probably a lot of Bingo players who make it."

"You think I will?...Make it into heaven?"

"You're a shoo-in, Mrs. Watkins. You'll be at the head of the line."

"I've done lots of...bad things, you know. Really bad. All those things I accused Roger of, I did the. . ."

"First of all," said Edward, "I find it very hard to believe you've done a lot of bad things. The second thing is that people with good hearts always get in. Always. And you've got a very good heart, Mrs. Watkins."

"My, my...Maybe I will come down after dinner for Bingo," she said. "Might as well practice up."

Edward rolled the cart toward the door.

"I'll be expecting some poetry next week," he said. "Don't forget."

"Maybe I'll write about the Bingo players in heaven," she said.

"Perfect," said Edward.

"...Look, the birds are coming back to the feeder."

"I know...Have a peaceful evening."

"Yes. I believe I will."

Bravo, said Sarah. Well done. Soon you won't need me at all.

Not so fast, said Edward. Seems to me we're going through the easy part of all this. What happens when we have to bring all this to some kind of conclusion? Huh? Some resolution. What happens to poor crazy Mrs. Reardon and David Sparrowhawk and the rest of them? We just leave them hanging out there?

No, Edward. They'll be taken care of. All things in good

74

time. Just trust. That's one of your lessons, too. No one will be abandoned at a crucial time. Someone is watching the Store. Believe me.

CHAPTER 10

Edward's young son, Steve, stood behind the couch and examined the back of his father's head where the hair was thinning. He carefully parted the few remaining strands and looked closely at the scalp.

"Hair's falling out, daddy."

"I know, Stevie. I'm doing my best to hold on to it."

"It doesn't look good without hair."

"My head doesn't?"

"Yeah."

"I know. Doesn't feel good either."

"What happens if it all falls out?"

"...Nothing," said Edward. "Why should anything happen?"

"Do you die when all your hair falls out?"

"No," said Edward. "Did somebody tell you that?"

"Frankie's daddy died and he didn't have any hair."

"Frankie's dad was killed in a car accident. Didn't have anything to do with his hair."

"Oh," said Steve. "If I had a comb, I could fix your hair. Make it look good."

Edward dug in his back pocket, retrieved a comb and handed it over his shoulder. Steve ever so gently combed the hair on the side toward the top and patted it in place. Edward loved the touch of the tiny hands on his head.

"Hair's all wet," said Steve.

"I just took a shower."

"Mommy dries her hair with that blower thing."

"Women do that sometimes."

"A brush would be better," he said. "Can we use Mommy's brush?"

"If she doesn't catch us."

Steve's voice dropped to a whisper.

"What happens if she catches us?"

"We might have to go to our rooms," said Edward.

The comb stopped in mid stroke.

"…You, too?" said Steve.

"Sometimes."

A broad grin crossed Steve's face.

"Wow," he said.

"Go ahead and get the brush. We'll take a chance."

Steve padded quickly into the bathroom, retrieved a brush from the countertop, hurried back behind the couch and started to brush Edward's hair.

"You got some gray hair, too, daddy."

"Lots?"

"No. Only a little."

"That's a relief," said Edward.

"Mommy says people get gray hair when they get old."

"…Or when they can't afford hair coloring," he said quietly.

"Can't what?"

"Nothing, son. Just thinking out loud."

"Are you old, daddy?"

"Well, depends on how you look at it. You, pal, might think I'm old because you're very young. On the other hand, if my father were alive, he'd think I was young."

"...What does that mean?"

"It means no, I'm not very old."

"How old do you have to be to be old."

Those kind of questions just warm my heart, said Sarah.

That's because you don't have to answer them, said Edward. And don't you have be human to have a heart?

Oh, you earthlings and your details. Besides, I was human. And more than once by the way. I've had lots of hearts.

I bet they were all very small, said Edward.

...Sigh...Carry on, Edward.

"How old do you think would be old?" said Edward.

"...Thirty?"

"Well, I'm fifty, and I don't think that's very old..."

"Wow. Fifty...Is Mommy that old?"

"No...How old are you, Stevie?"

"Oh, you know. Seven almost eight."

"Seven almost eight, eh?" said Edward.

"Almost..."

Steve was quiet for a few moments, attending to the task of brushing his father's hair.

"...Are you gonna die soon, daddy?"

Edward turned and lifted his young son over the back of the couch onto his lap.

"My goodness, pal, what's all this about gray hair and getting old and dying?"

Steve leaned against his father's chest and played with the brush.

"Frankie's daddy wasn't as old as you even, and he died."

"Sometimes when accidents happen people die sooner... than maybe they should."

"Is that what happened to Tommy?"

"...Right. That's what happened to Tommy."

"What happens after you die?"

My, my, such hard questions, said Sarah.

"You go on to. . .another life."
"Mommy said we go to heaven when we die," said Steve.
"Mommy said that?"
"Is that what happens? We go to heaven?"
"Well. . .Yes. I think that's exactly right. Absolutely. We go to heaven."
"Is it nice there? In heaven?"
"Oh, yeah. Really nice."
". . .Where is it?"
"Where's heaven?"
"Yeah."
"Isn't it your bedtime, pal?"
"Daddy," he scolded. "We didn't even have dinner yet."
"Oh, right. Well. . .Heaven is far away. Far, far away."
"Like Wyoming?"
"Even farther," said Edward.
"Wow. . .Do they have trees there?"
"Yeah. Great trees," said Edward.
"I could put my swing in a tree."
"You could do that."
"Mommy says there's angels there. . .In heaven."

Good for Mommy, said Sarah. At least somebody in the family knows what's happening.

"Angels," said Edward. "I'm sure there are. I think actually, they. . ."
"Dinner, boys," Pam called from the kitchen. "Come-and-get-it."
Steve scooted off his lap, dashed into the bathroom and set the brush down on the counter. He emerged with a

conspiratorial grin on his face, pulled his father off the couch and held his hand as they marched off to dinner.

. . .*Left, right, left, right, said Sarah.*

Edward just shook his head.

CHAPTER 11

Most Friday afternoons at the Hospice there was
entertainment, usually provided by local musicians from the
nearby Folklore Center. Occasionally someone would show up
and do a travelog, complete with slides and narration, but it was
mostly musicians who provided the entertainment. Though
there were a few professionals among them, most were young
students from the Center hoping to sharpen their skills on a
captive audience. Guitar players, dulcimer players, mandolin,
piano and fiddle players. Most were unprepared for the nearly
total lack of attention they received. Many of the patients talked
to loved ones long absent, some hummed or sang songs that
bore no resemblance to what was being played, a few who were
heavily sedated simply fell asleep, others waved their arms
about, singing *tra la la, tra la la*, because they didn't know the
words. Requests for songs nearly always went unfilled; few of
the musicians knew songs like "Don't Bring Lulu" or "Poor
Little Rich Girl." Despite the distractions, the musicians kept
coming; most learned that it helped to have a sense of humor.

Mr. Barnett always came when there was a piano player,

hoping to hear some blues or barrelhouse or some stride. Maybe even some jazz, though he had given up expecting too much. But sometimes he was pleasantly surprised. Not often, but sometimes. So he kept coming.

Mr. Barnett used a hand-held voice box to talk because cancer had stolen his ability to speak. There was a hole in his throat (always covered by an elegant red scarf) where his larynx and vocal chords used to be. He didn't like using the voice box because he knew it made him sound like a badly modulated, computerized imitation of a human voice—garbled and hard to understand. He had been a talker in his pre-cancer days, a spinner of urban tales, of magic, a raconteur who could capture and hold an audience with his voice, a man who painted pictures with words. Without the words, his life had become a barren landscape without color or texture. He was dying as much from his inability to speak as he was from the cancer itself. Now he was mostly reduced to writing notes. The only times he attempted to talk were when he spoke to the nurses, or to one of the piano players. But names like Porkchops Green, Champion Jack Dupree or Cripple Clarence Lofton seldom drew anything but blank stares from the budding musicians. Mr. Barnett held little hope that the younger generation would amount to much.

And of course, Mrs. Mathews was always there, vigorously tapping her foot or singing along when the occasion presented itself, *tra la la-ing* when the words got away from her (which they often did). She knew many of the songs, but could not recall the lyrics with any clarity; the words just seemed to congregate in the center of her head and come out in a random fashion. The cancer gathered like storm clouds in her brain, casting shadows over normal functions, sometimes making speech unintelligible. But even the *tra la las* sounded good to her; singing was such a joyful experience. Lately she had been subject to sudden, unexpected attacks of nausea, throwing up without warning. The nurses gave her a barf bag to carry with her, but she could never remember what it was for until it was too late. One day she threw up on Mr. Ambrose's new chrome walker; it took him a week to get over it, (muttering curses and thumping along with his walker), though she forgot almost immediately. And she didn't understand why Mr. Ambrose seemed so mad at her.

Mrs. McKelvey attended whenever she could, her wheelchair usually in the front row, waving her arms about as if she were conducting an orchestra, singing with gusto if she had just had her orange juice and bourbon, otherwise just humming along.

Mr. Ambrose came with his chrome walker, requesting Big Band songs by Benny Gladman or King Stutz, or at least something from the War.

"'Praise the Lord and Pass the Bullets.' You know that one?...'We Done It Before And We Can Do It Again'?"

"...Sorry, sir."

"How about 'When Johnny Comes Marchin' Home?' That was from another War, entirely different from this one lately. It was called The Great War, the War to end all Wars. Can you imagine that?...What would all the young people do without wars?"

Miss Gladys always wanted to hear "The Old Rugged Cross," which many of the musicians knew, but Official Hospice Policy was that songs of a religious nature should be discouraged outside of formal chapel services. Ever since an unfortunate incident involving an overzealous Christian volunteer actually baptizing an old Jewish lady on her deathbed, Father Tom had been very strict about what he considered religious meddling. Especially since the family, nearly all lawyers, had walked in on the ceremony just as Grandma was being thrust into the bosom of Jesus.

Father Tom was very big on religious freedom. He was considered something of a loose cannon by the more orthodox members of the Christian community.

83

"If you come here as a Buddhist," he was fond of saying, "it would be our pleasure to have you leave as a Buddhist."

He eventually took to interviewing the prospective volunteers himself, hoping to detect Evangelical Christians baptizing their way to salvation before they could do any damage.

When he wasn't tending the garden, Eldon stopped by to listen, closing his eyes and smiling, as if he knew something no one else knew.

"The Great Pumpkin is growing in the garden," he would say cryptically, smiling that smile, nodding to himself. "Oh, yes. Where the grapes of wrath make honey wine."

"Praise Jesus," said Miss Gladys, never one to miss an opportunity for praise.

"There's a pumpkin somewhere?" said Mrs. McKelvey. "In the garden?"

"O Great Pumpkin," said Eldon, "grant your children abundance, sunflowers the size of Frisbees, tulips like coffee cups."

"I never noticed a pumpkin in the garden."

"Only the children can see it."

". . .Praise Jesus."

"It's like the Garden at Findhorn out there," said Eldon. "You ever hear about that place? Daisies big as plates. Angels, Elementals and Devas everywhere…Have you seen the garden, Mr. Ambrose?"

"…Give My Regrets To Broadway," said Mr. Ambrose. "You remember that movie?"

"What movie was that?"

"About the Broadwalk. Atlantic City I believe. Burt Lanchester and some babe…I forget what it was about, but the Lanchester guy was old. Old and sad, which is usually the way it is. Me? I'm an exception. The babe was young." He pondered that for a moment. "He died…Then she left. That's the way it was. Sometimes it happens the other way around. But not

84

often."

Mrs. Reardon inched her way from her room toward the Lounge, creeping along slowly in her wheelchair, glancing suspiciously up and down the hallway.

"They're coming," she said. "Sure as shit. Through the windows, up from the basement…they're coming and we'll all be killed. Sure as shit."

Mary Blanchard came sailing up the corridor, a symphony in white in her starched nurse's uniform.

"I do declare, it's Mrs. Reardon," she said. "Look like you gettin' on pretty good."

Mrs. Reardon stopped moving, folded her hands in her lap and sat quietly, waiting for the storm to pass.

"You goin' to the concert?" said Mary. "I hear they got a good piano player."

Mrs. Reardon closed her eyes and tried to act invisible.

"You want some help, honey? I be glad to push you on down to the Lounge."

Mrs. Reardon took a deep breath and spoke slowly.

"There are people coming in the windows, Nurse. Poison gas is being released through the radiators in the basement. . . and you want to know if I'd like help getting to the Lounge?"

"We be takin' care of all that," said Mary. "The poison gas and the people comin' in the windows? We got Mr. Bill on it."

"…Mr. Bill?" said Mrs. Reardon. "And who might Mr. Bill be?"

"Maintenance."

"Ah, maintenance," she said, nodding. "That explains everything. Maintenance. Of course. Mr. Bill, the Maintenance Man."

"He be takin' care of things."

"Mr. Bill is just one person? He doesn't have helpers?"

"Not any to mention," said Mary.

"God, it's a wonder we're still alive," said Mrs. Reardon. "And no matter what you've heard, Nurse, I am not now, nor have I ever been, a member of the Communist Party. Or a prostitute...Did you know that I slept with Jack Kennedy?"

"No," said Mary, gently beginning to push the wheelchair toward the Lounge. "I never heard that."

"Yes...And I wasn't the only one."

"That right?"

"But I never got paid...never..."

"That man had plenty money," said Mary. "You be doin' it for love?"

Mrs. Reardon smiled ever so slightly.

"You could say that," she said. "I mean that's accurate, as far as it goes. But he wasn't much. Not when you consider who he was."

"Where'd you meet?"

"The Zebra Room."

"You ever hear that old blues tune, 'I'm a One Hour Woman, Got Me a Five Minute Man'? You ever hear that?"

Mrs. Reardon giggled, though the sound that came out was more like a cough.

"Oh," she said. "...Oh, that's good."

"And true," said Mary.

"Yes."

They rolled slowly passed Room 109 where the Borsteins were quartered.

"How are the two old lovebirds?" said Mrs. Reardon.

"Doin' fine," said Mary.

But in fact, Mrs. Borstein had taken a bad fall when getting out of bed two days before, and, though there didn't appear to any broken bones, she had lain without speaking or moving ever since. Recently her vital signs had begun to weaken. Mr. Borstein knew she was fading when she didn't show any interest in watching Jeopardy, a game they had played together for years. . .Honey? . .Honey? . .Literature, your favorite category. You okay? You need me I'll come over there. . .But he couldn't spend much time in his wheelchair, so mostly he watched from his bed a few feet away, listened to the shallow breathing become shallower until he had to strain to hear it at all. He watched helplessly as his wife prepared to die.

"...They be doin' just fine," said Mary.

"Been married a long time, haven't they?"

"Sixty years."

"I couldn't imagine being married for sixty years," said Mrs. Reardon. "At least not to one man. Men are so...boring after awhile. Don't you think?"

"Different strokes, honey," said Mary.

"They have these...tricks they do. You know—weenie tricks. And after they show you all the tricks, they leave. They find someone else who might be interested. Weenie tricks. God. . .They think they have to show it to everyone. Who cares?"

It was Mary's turn to laugh.

Mrs. Reardon spied Edward pushing the Cocktail Cart down the corridor.

"Oh, there...Time for a drink?" she said.

"I believe so," said Edward.

"Do you think you could locate some vodka and tomato juice on that stupid cart? Maybe some celery and radishes? A Bloody Mary for Bloody Mary Reardon."

"I don't know about the celery and radishes, but I think we can locate some vodka and tomato juice."

She suddenly stiffened and grabbed at the wheels to stop the wheelchair.

"You hear that?" she whispered.

Mary and Edward exchanged glances.

"Hear what?" said Mary.

"That...that hissing sound. It's the poison gas in the basement. Didn't I tell you? First the gas, then they'll be coming in through the windows. We'll all be killed. You won't like that part, Nurse. . .And not even Buffalo Bill the Maintenance Man, or all the King's horses or all the King's men will be able to save us."

"We've got some Absolut Vodka today, Mrs. Reardon. Supposed to be very good stuff. Very expensive."

"About time," she said, momentarily distracted from her paranoia. "I've been getting the cheap stuff all my life. Bargain Basement Reardon. You remember that song—'Second Hand Rose'? That's my style. Everything's on sale—everything. Including me. I'm on my way to a concert now. A piano concert? Isn't that right, Nurse?. .Of course we may not live long enough to get there. Not the way things are going. Unless Buffalo Bill can save us. But then nobody gives a rat's ass anyway."

"Better have that drink before we get to the Lounge," said Mary. "You know how Father Tom is about food and drink and the new carpet."

"Father Tom," said Mrs. Reardon, shaking her head. "God's little helper." She watched as Edward measured out a single shot of vodka. "Oh, come now," she said. "Put some vodka in it."

Edward splashed a little more in the glass, added the tomato juice and handed it to her.

"No celery? No radishes. . ?"

"Hard times," said Edward. "Cutbacks. Layoffs. You know how it is."

"Just my luck," she said. "I end up in the Slammer just when the Depression hits."

They continued on toward the Lounge. Mrs. Reardon downed her Bloody Mary before they had gone twenty feet.

"Catherine the Great drank vodka," she said. "For breakfast. And she didn't do too bad."

The first song they heard was "You Are My Sunshine." Though she had initially started out with the right words, Mrs. Mathews had slipped sideways into a chorus of "On Top of Old Smoky." Mrs. McKelvey was bravely trying to stay with the original song and Mr. Ambrose was wavering somewhere between the two, throwing in a loud baritone *Huzzah!* when it seemed appropriate. Mary marched up toward the piano, belting out a chorus of "You Are My Sunshine," dragging the singers along with her by the sheer force of her voice. Mr. Barnett smiled, appreciating the style. He put the voice modulator to his neck.

"Migh-ty fine," he said in that mechanical monotone.

"I need another drink," said Mrs. Reardon.

"Tomorrow," said Edward.

"Not everyone has a tomorrow," she said. "Don't forget that."

. . .Did you hear that? said Sarah.

I did, said Edward.

It's worth remembering. Tomorrow's just a word; today is all there really is. For everyone. . .

Later that evening, the Borstein family was called and the Vigil began for Mrs. Borstein. Mr. Borstein fought to stay awake, struggling against the morphine and the dull pain that coursed just below the surface. Sons and daughters, grandchildren, even two of the great grandchildren gathered around the bed as Mrs. Borstein began the final few steps of her earthly journey.

Mr. Borstein was apparently the only one who noticed the figure surrounded by light at the foot of his bed. Bright as it was, he couldn't understand why everyone didn't see it. They just acted as if nothing was happening. He wanted to tell them, but discovered he couldn't speak. The figure, which could have been either male or female, beckoned with a broad smile. Mr. Borstein was enveloped by a tremendous sense of peace. He felt himself being lifted out of the bed, though he was sure his body was still there, and moving toward the light. It was all so effortless. He thought he said Angel out loud, but he wasn't sure. When he got to where the figure was, he looked back at himself on the bed...where he seemed to be sleeping peacefully.

Is that me? he said.
That's the body you used while you were on earth.
...But it's not me?
No, said Sarah. Not anymore. You're here with me.
That mean I'm ...dead?
That's what people on earth call it.
But I'm not?
Do you feel dead?
...No. I feel different. Free somehow. ..What about Millie?
She'll be along in a minute. Watch. Your family is about to discover that you're gone.

Just then his oldest son Milt turned toward his bed and placed a hand gently on his shoulder.

"Did you say something, Dad?...Something about an angel?"

When there was no reply, he leaned over and put his ear next to his father's chest for perhaps fifteen seconds, then straightened up and rang the call button. When Vivian arrived, he said:

"I think he's having a...bad time. I don't think he's breathing."

Vivian leaned over, looked at the eyes, put her fingers to the side of his neck.

A few moments later she said, "He's gone."

"...Dead?" said Milt. "He's dead? How can he be dead? I was just talking to him. Mom's the one who. . ." His eyes begged for an explanation.

"It happens very quickly sometimes," she said.

"But you could. . .revive him? With those paddle things? Like they have on ER?"

"That's not what we do here," she said gently. "We let them go when it's time."

"But you could...do something, couldn't you? To bring him back."

"Do you think your father would want to come back?" Milt looked at the withered figure on the bed.

I sure wish somebody would close my mouth, said Mr. Borstein. Or pull the sheet up. I look absolutely terrible.

Oh, it's a nice old body, said Sarah. Served you well for eighty years.

Milt didn't speak for awhile.

"No," he said finally. "I don't think he would." He looked at Vivian with her halo of gray hair. For a moment she looked like an angel.

I'm here, Milt, said Mr. Borstein. Everything's okay. Mom's coming along soon.

He can't hear you, said Sarah. . .As soon as Mildred gets here, we'll head for the Life Review Room and look at some film.

Film of what?

Of your life. Your entire life has been recorded, though not really on film as you think of film. That's just what we call it.

Lord, I don't know if I'm gonna like this. I haven't been all that good a person. . .There's been times when. . .

It's about lessons, not punishment, said Sarah. That punishment thing got started eons ago and we can't seem to shake it loose. . .You'll be getting ready for your next trip back to earth. Going over the lessons you've learned, deciding what you want to work on next time.

Going back to earth? said Mr. Borstein. I'll be coming back here?

Yes. We'll pick a time period, your gender, your parents,

91

the lessons you'd like to learn.

. . .What happened to heaven?

Oh. . .It's just a handy word, said Sarah. Don't worry, you'll be losing your Earth Mentality soon and you'll start to remember the Big Picture.

Lord, said Mr. Borstein. . .Here comes Millie.

. . .Harry? said Mrs. Borstein.

Millie. . .

And off we go to Life Review, said Sarah.

Vivian pulled the sheet up over Mr. Borstein and put her arms around Milt.

"The strangest thing," he said. "I could have sworn I heard him say Angel just before he died."

Vivian smiled.

"Very possible," she said. "He's in good hands now."

CHAPTER 12

Mr. Ambrose was constantly on the move, thumping up and down the hallways with his walker, plodding relentlessly onward for hours at a time. Hair sprouted from his ears and his nose, as wild and unruly as the hair on his head. His maroon smoking jacket, a constant article of attire, was badly stained and in need of cleaning. The nursing staff wondered how he kept going, hour after hour, day after day. After all, he had advanced stomach cancer and he was seventy-five years of age. When Tony asked him why he kept walking and didn't sit down to rest, he confided that it was the piles.

"Hemorrhoids?" said Tony.

"…Piles," said Mr. Ambrose.

"You know we have an inflatable donut you can sit on."

"A donut you sit on?…That helps?"

"It's like a life preserver," said Tony. "Little plastic thing filled with air. Like a donut…with a hole in the middle. Relieves the pressure on your…piles."

"Huh," said Mr. Ambrose. "A donut, eh?"

"Donut shaped. Round…with a hole in the middle. I've got

one down in the office. Want to try it?"

"You sit on it?"

"Right. Only the part that's tender? That part doesn't have any pressure on it. Doesn't touch anything. It's over the hole in the donut."

Mr. Ambrose looked down the length of the hall.

"Maybe I'll try that someday," he said. "That donut thing. Might be a good idea. Just might work out fine."

He began to move away slowly, thumping the walker forward, following it with two short steps.

"Not right now, though. Got a busy day. No sittin' down today. Have to check things. Mr. Bill depends on me to keep an eye on things. Says he can't trust the women."

"I understand you're a member of the Volunteer Fire Department."

"I watch for things," said Mr. Ambrose. "Keep my eye out. I was a night watchman once."

"He told me how much help you were."

"He did, eh?"

"Oh, yes," said Tony. "Told me he wouldn't know how to get along without your help."

"Huh…That Mr. Bill's a pretty sharp fella."

Mr. Ambrose always ordered Diet Pepsi and gin when the Cocktail Cart came around.

"How come Diet Pepsi and not Regular?" said Edward.

Mr. Ambrose rubbed his stomach.

"Regular's tough on the stomach."

Edward asked him if it had a name, the Pepsi and gin drink.

"I call it a Piggy," he said. "Named it after my first wife."

"That was her name? Piggy?"

"No, Peggy. Piggy's just what I called her."

"Oh…" Edward wanted to ask what she called him, but

thought better of it.

"I was married twice more. Twice after Piggy. You got a wife?"

"I do," said Edward. "Pam."

"First one?"

"Second."

"Kids?"

"Two. Steven. . .and Tommy."

"How old?"

"Stevie's almost eight and Tommy...Tommy would have been twenty-eight or nine."

"Tommy's...not here no more?" said Mr. Ambrose.

"No."

"Dead?"

"Yeah," said Edward.

"I know about that. About kids leavin'...dyin'. How'd it happen?"

Edward gripped the edge of the Cocktail Cart.

"Rolled his car..." he said. "His pickup truck. Out on Highway 10 between Blythe and Phoenix. Mile marker sixty-five. Broke his neck."

"Arizona, eh," said Mr. Ambrose, shaking his head. "I lived in Arizona once. Bisbee. . ."

"Bisbee..."

"East of Tucson. After the war. Moved as far away from the ocean as I could."

Edward took a deep breath and exhaled slowly.

"...I bet," he said.

"You ever eat what they used to call Spam?"

"I don't know. Maybe a long time ago." He relaxed his grip on the Cart when he felt it tilt.

"Not bad. Made from leftovers. They sweep up the floor in the butcher shop, mash it all in a little square and put it in a tin can. S'all we ate during the War. We'd put cloves in it and pretend it was ham. But it didn't taste no better...You

95

remember the War?"

"World War II?"

"Yeah."

"Hard to forget World War II," said Edward.

"I was in it. In the War. Under Patton. Eleventh Armored Division. Battle of the Bulge." He chuckled at the memory. "Hitler's SS Troops. Panzers. Ha! We had 'em on the run. I was married to Piggy then. She stayed home, and I went to War. That's the way we did it in those days. 'Cept I almost ended up with two wives there for awhile when I was in England. Me and Jilly Johnson got chummy for awhile. She worked in a factory, Piggy did. Built airplanes. We even had a baby. Jesus God, babies."

He coughed and shook his head.

"First one was a boy. Teddy. Theodore Runyan Ambrose. Family name. Then two girls—Paulette and Teresa, but I had a different wife then. Martha, I think. Maybe Esther…You ever heard of sittin' on a donut? For piles?"

"I have," said Edward.

"It supposed to help?"

"That's what they say. Relieves the pressure."

"That's what the Big Guy said."

"Tony?"

"I suppose…You know, piles is the worse curse ever sent to mankind. Gotta be a cruel God would do a thing like that, like piles. Have people suffer like that. I got serious stomach problems not as bad as piles. Jesus…"

"Well, I hear those donut things really help."

"I believe I'll try one—one of them donut things. I could prob'ly do that, sit on it. You think?"

"I don't see why not," said Edward. "That why you stand up a lot? Because of the piles?"

"Oh, no," said Mr. Ambrose. "I'm just a goer. Guy on the move. Never been much for sittin'."

"Oh. . ."

"You don't think it'd look stupid or anything, me sittin' on a donut like that?"

"No. People do it all the time. Matter of fact, you can't even see it when you're sitting on it."

"That so? I could try it."

"Can't hurt," said Edward.

"You sure that's Diet Pepsi?" said Mr. Ambrose, indicating the can Edward was opening.

Edward glanced at it.

"Diet Pepsi it is," he said.

"You know I can tell the difference between Diet and Regular. Not many people can do that. Used to be I could tell the difference between VO and Canadian Club. Blindfolded. In the old days. But I had to quit drinking whiskey. Bad for my stomach."

Edward poured a healthy shot of Silver Slipper Gin into a plastic tumbler, added ice, a splash of Pepsi and handed it to Mr. Ambrose.

"Gin's better for you than whiskey," he said. "Got juniper berries in it. That's what the Indians used for stomach aches. Juniper berries. Them Indians knew a lot."

"Really."

"Juniper berries and tree bark. Eucalyptus bark. That's what they make aspirin from. And that's why Indians never get headaches. Bet you didn't know that, eh?"

"I didn't."

Mr. Ambrose held up his drink in a toast.

"Here's lookin' at you, kid," he said. "…That's from a movie, that line. Here's lookin' at you, kid. Remember?"

"Sure. Casablanca."

"Harry Bogart and that foreign broad."

Mr. Ambrose tried to smooth his hair with his right hand.

"My hair look okay?"

"Terrific."

"I gotta get my jacket cleaned," said Mr. Ambrose. "Got

stains all over it."

"That was Ingrid Bergman."

"...What was Ingrid Bergman?"

"In Casablanca. The foreign broad."

"I knew that. Ingrid Bergman. Yeah. A hot number, eh?"

"Very hot," said Edward.

"Boy, what I couldn't do with a hot number," said Mr. Ambrose. He took a sip of his drink. "You like movies?"

"Love movies."

"I musta seen most every movie made. I useta hide in the movies when I was a kid."

"Me, too," said Edward.

"That was when they had George Raft and Timmy Cagney and those guys. Garfold and Bogart and Barbara Standoff and the rest. Real movie stars, not like these jerks today. I remember most every movie I ever saw. I got a great memory. People used to remark on it. What a memory. Gigantic. I got the memory of a person twice my age."

"What's the best movie you ever saw?"

Mr. Ambrose rubbed the side of his face.

"...One would be How Green Was My Valley. Great movie. Wally Pidgeon and somebody else. They Died With Their Boots On. Rudolph Scott, I think. That was good. And that new one, On The Waterfront, Merlo Brandon and some other guys I like. Lee Cobb was in it. Karl Madden...Some broad with a saint's name."

"Great movies," said Edward.

"Yeah. I coulda been a contendah. Remember that?"

"Sure."

"You know I heard those people in 109...passed on. The twins?"

"Married couple," said Edward. "The Borsteins. They just looked alike. They...left within minutes of each other."

"Huh," said Mr. Ambrose. "Strange, eh? I mean dyin' like that, so close together."

"Yeah..."

"That happen often, you think? Dyin' like that?"

"I don't think so."

"Huh...What's your favorite movie?"

"One is Fat City," said Edward. "John Huston movie about a drunken ex-pug trying to make a comeback."

"I seen it," said Mr. Ambrose, slapping the walker. "Tracy Whatshisname, eh?"

Edward hesitated for a moment.

"...Right. *Stacy. Stacy* Keach. Remember who played the young fighter?"

Mr. Ambrose rattled his walker as if to shake up his memory.

"...Don't tell me. Big family. Actors. All boys..."

"Right," said Edward. "One of the Bridges boys."

"Ha!" he said triumphantly. "I knew it. How's that for a memory, eh? Pulled it right out of the old sock. Helluva movie. 'Member how it ends? Just the two of 'em sittin' there havin' a cup of coffee, lookin' off somewhere in the air. Not sayin' anything. Hell, there ain't nothin' left to say..."

"Yeah. My other favorite movie is The Empire Strikes Back."

"That the one about The Force?...Dark Vader and all them?"

"Yeah."

"...Passable," Mr. Ambrose said cautiously. "I'm not partial to movies with things zippin' all over, goin' too fast. It's not like real life...The Force and all." He shook his head.

"You didn't like that part? The part about The Force?"

"No. The Force or that little dwarf guy...Yodo?"

"Yoda," said Edward.

"Right. Didn't care much for them fellas."

You know, Edward, you're turning out to be a much better student than I thought you'd be.

99

Doesn't feel like I'm such a good student. I don't know if you've noticed, but I resist a lot of this stuff. I tend to be. . . stubborn about things. Some things.

Oh, the best students are always stubborn, said Sarah. The best students ask questions and then struggle with the answers. That's how they learn.

"So what was it about The Force you didn't like?" said Edward.

"Oh...it all seemed phony. The Force and all. Obi Kenobi. Nothin' like that could happen."

"You don't think so?"

"No...You might not guess that I was at one time a church person. Regular. Went every week. Sometimes twice a week. Said prayers. Lots of prayers. Didn't do much good, but I said 'em anyway. Like I was told."

"Your folks were churchgoers?"

"That's how it started. They went so we went. Couldn't hardly stay home when we were little. But I kept goin' after I grew up, till after the War. Didn't make much sense then. Not after the War. People killin' each other. You shoulda seen it. Then the babies started dyin'. First Teddy, then Paulette... Wasn't no Force lookin' out after them now, was there? Wasn't no God Almighty Jesus Perfect Christ lookin' after them babies, was there?"

"I don't know," said Edward.

"I tell you a secret...nobody knows. Not them preachers, not them book writers. Nobody. They just say it's God's Will and everybody's in a better place. 'Cept they all look like they been suckin' on lemons when they say it. *Your babies are with Jesus now.* . .Like that's supposed to mean somethin'. They go to school and study up on what God is, but when it's all said and done, ain't nobody I know come back from the other side to say how really good it was and let's all hurry over there. You know anybody's come back and said how good a place it was?"

100

"...No."

Hey, what about me? said Sarah.
You don't count, said Edward. I mean you haven't actually come back, not like we're talking about. Not like a real person.
I'm trying not to be offended.
Sorry...
It's okay. I'm taking into account that you're only a Level One.

"Damn straight," said Mr. Ambrose. "Ain't nobody knows. Not the Pope. Not Billy Graham. Nobody. Them preachers just wanna put a hand in your pocket and pull out some money. That's all. Ain't no big mystery to it. They just keep talkin' about God Almighty Jesus Perfect Christ until you put some money in the basket...Then they quit till next week."

Without warning, he slumped against the side of his walker. Edward moved to help him, but Mr. Ambrose waved him away.

"I'm okay," he said quickly. "Just slipped." He brushed at some dirt on the lapel of his maroon smoking jacket. "You suppose you could get this cleaned for me?"

"Sure," said Edward. "I'll take it when I leave today. Be back in a couple of days."

"It's my best jacket. You tell 'em be careful."

"I will."

"You know this was give to me by a lady friend. 'Bout ten years ago. When I was still goin' strong. Her name was Edna. Young broad. Couldn't a been but fifty or so. Hot...You suppose you could get that donut thing from the Big Guy?"

"I could ask. I'm sure it won't be a problem."

"You ever hear of a guy dyin' from a sore ass?" said Mr. Ambrose.

Edward treated the question in the same serious way it was asked.

101

"No, can't recall as I have. If you're in pain, let Tony know. Or one of the other nurses. They'll get something for you."

Mr. Ambrose ran his hand through his hair.

"Gotta get a haircut, too. They have people come in and do that?"

"Every Wednesday," said Edward.

...Ask him if he's still mad at God? said Sarah.

"You still mad at God?" said Edward.

"...Oh, I don't know if I was all that mad. It's just that it ain't right. Any fool could tell that. Babies dyin'. What kinda deal is that?"

. . .It might be the kind of deal where you get mad, said Sarah. Unless, of course, you knew..

Knew what? said Edward.

That nobody dies. Since dying is a Level One concept, it's quite normal to be angry about it.

You going to tell me about Tommy?

In good time, Edward.

But. . .

We've been over this. When you get ready to go to Level Two you'll begin to have some inkling that life simply goes on, that nobody really dies. Obviously you're not quite ready for that yet.

I thought you said I was a good student.

And so you are, said Sarah. But just because you're a good first grade student, it doesn't mean you're ready to go to college..

But why. . .

No, no, said Sarah. Not this Need-To-Know thing again. Acceptance, Edward. Trust. Be assured that all is well in the Kingdom. It's about lessons. Try to remember that. . .

102

"Doesn't sound like a great deal," said Edward.

"Wasn't," said Mr. Ambrose, wincing as he eased himself onto his bed. "Babies dyin's not a good deal no matter how you call it. Man's not supposed to outlive his kids. You know that." He shook his head.

Edward wheeled the Cocktail Cart toward the door.

"I'll get the donut from Tony," he said. "Believe me, it'll make your life better."

Mr. Ambrose was trying to find a comfortable spot to sit.

"Good," he said. "Anybody needs life to be a little better, it's yours truly."

CHAPTER 13

Nobody knew what to make of the call at first. Clark, the Charge Nurse on the afternoon shift, took the call and immediately went to Father Tom to tell him about it.

"Said his name was Little Bear and he would be down soon to pick up David Sparrowhawk."

"Did this Little Bear say who he was?"

"No. Just Little Bear."

"You didn't ask?"

"No. Didn't get a chance to. He just said he'd be down to pick up David soon and hung up."

"Well, look in the records and see if it's his father. My guess is that it is. Didn't his sister come with him when he was admitted?...Dawn something? Or something Dawn?"

"I wasn't here that day," said Clark, fussing with his bow tie.

"And go ask David his father's name. If it all checks out, get him ready to go. It's probably best for everyone."

"But...he has a catheter in and he's on lots of pain medication. He's going to need..."

"Take the catheter out, Clark. Give him some medication to take with him and have Doctor Seabert write out a perscription for whatever else he may need. And give him one of those big boxes of diapers."

"But can he just do that? Just walk out when he's in the middle of…you know."

"Of dying?"

"Well, yeah."

"Of course he can. We didn't capture him, Clark. He's not our prisoner. He can go anywhere he wants. With our blessing. We are not privy to any special communication from God about the matter. Perhaps he is. He may need to die somewhere else. Who knows? Just be sure Tony gets him to sign the usual release form."

"…Right," said Clark. "Of course. What am I thinking about?"

They were in the process of getting him ready when Edward arrived at his room to take him out for a smoke. He stood at the doorway for a moment and watched.

"Getting ready for a party?" said Edward.

"Goin' home, Paleface," he said. "Just like you said. Goin' home. Hard to believe one of you guys was tellin' the truth."

"Great," said Edward.

You seem surprised, said Sarah. . .Oh ye of little faith. Didn't I tell you? Didn't I say he wouldn't die here?

I believed you, Edward protested.

My angelic tush you believed me. No way in the world you thought it was actually going to happen.

. . .But I did consider the possibility that it might happen. To my credit, I did consider that.

Never mind, Paleface, said Sarah.

"My father's comin' to get me," said David. "Little Bear."

"Little Bear," said Edward, smiling.

105

"Goin' back to the reservation. To my people. To live there for…for as long as there is."

The nurses got him into his treasured blue jacket (next to his Nike shoes, his most prized possession). Edward helped him into the wheelchair and pushed him out front to wait in the Smoking Room. Tony brought a box of diapers, a Kmart shopping bag with David's prescription drugs and personal possessions and set them by the door. He knelt next to the wheelchair and gave David an awkward hug.

"Journey well, David."

"I will."

"We'll meet again," said Tony.

"I know," said David.

Tony gave Edward the note with all the information about necessary medications.

"I'll be back when his father gets here," said Tony. "He'll need to sign the release form."

After Tony left, they sat in silence for a few moments.

"Well, how's it feel to be going home?" said Edward.

David blew a smoke ring and stuck his index finger through the hole.

"…Unreal," said David. "Like it can't really be happening. You realize I'm goin' home to die, man."

"I know," said Edward. "It seems like a very…brave thing to do."

"It does?"

"Yeah."

"Huh…Brave me. Who would'a thought?" He shook his head. "I wonder why this is all happening now? I mean goin' home and everything."

"I don't know," said Edward. "First I knew about it was this afternoon when I came to take you out for a smoke."

"You didn't fix it?…Didn't call my father? Talk him into comin' to get me?"

"No."

106

"Who did?"

"I don't have a clue," said Edward. "Maybe he just decided by himself."

"Maybe...Here I was goin' to give you credit for all this and now I find out that it happened all by itself."

. . .Here, here, said Sarah. Nothing just happens by itself. You earthlings, sometimes I wonder. There is meaning and purpose to everything. Everything. Not knowing what it is does not indicate a lack of meaning. Coincidence? No-o-o-o-o. . . The Great Spirit, or whatever you choose to call It, has a hand in everything. . .Is everything, actually.

Should I tell him all that? said Edward.

No. He'll find out soon enough. Just tell him whatever seems appropriate.

"...Actually I did fix it," said Edward. "Set the whole thing up myself."

. . .I should have known, said Sarah. . .

"But you just said you didn't even know about it," said David.

"Doesn't stop me from wanting to take credit for it."

"You Palefaces," he said. He lit another cigarette and rubbed his front teeth with his index finger. "Still bleedin'?"

"Not much," said Edward. "Just a little red. Looks like you've been eating cherries."

"Fat chance..."

David watched the smoke from his cigarette curl up toward the ceiling.

"I didn't see Cowboy yesterday," he said. "Or today...That mean he's gone?"

"That's what they tell me," said Edward. "They came to get him for dinner and he was...gone."

"Old Cowboy," said David, squinting through the smoke. "Dead and gone. The Last Roundup. He was a pistol...We used to talk, me and him. The Cowboy and the Indian."

"You did?"

"Yeah."

"They tell me he could sing," said Edward.

"I only heard him sing that one about The Last Roundup."

"Old Gene Autry song."

". . .Gene who?" said David.

"Movie cowboy. Gene Autry, Roy Rogers. Hopalong Cassidy. You know."

"We never saw any cowboy movies."

"They show them on teevee all the time," said Edward. "Late night teevee."

"We never had a teevee."

"Well...You didn't miss much anyway."

David flicked his ashes in the general direction of the large ashtray.

"...Sometimes I wonder what happened to General Custard after he died."

"What's your best guess?" said Edward.

"I think he went and got AIDS. Somewhere in the Afterlife. And he's the only one that's got it. Everybody else gets cured when they get there, but he actually gets infected. First time that's ever happened...He has to wear a bell around his neck so that people can hear him coming. Isn't that what you Christians did to the lepers? Didn't they have to shout *Unclean! Unclean!* so that everyone would know they were lepers? So nobody would get too close? That's what I think happened to Custard. If there's any justice at all, that's what happened."

"Hope they don't put you in charge of the Afterlife," said Edward. "No one will ever get in."

"What's fair's fair, man. Justice. . ."

David leaned forward and looked at his shoes.

"You want to tie these again, man? You're the only one gets it right."

"That's why they pay me the big bucks," he said. "We've spared no expense to make sure your shoes are tied right."

He was tying David's shoes when the pickup truck pulled up in front of the Hospice. When he looked up, Little Bear was framed in the doorway. He was of medium height, slightly built, dressed in Levi pants and a faded blue shirt, his hair long, dark, tied in a ponytail. Just behind him was a young Native American woman about David's age.

Edward finished tying the shoes and got to his feet.

"David," said Little Bear.

"...Papa," said David.

"Time to come home."

David nodded without speaking.

Without even glancing at Edward, Little Bear came forward, easily lifted his son out of the wheelchair and carried him to the pickup truck. The bed of the old Ford truck was covered with two long rolls of egg-crate foam that would serve as a mattress. Edward picked up the box of diapers, the Kmart bag and followed them outside. A black mongrel dog in the truck stood guard and barked as they approached.

"Hello, Chief," said David, setting the dog's tail in motion. "You must be a hundred years old by now."

The woman smiled shyly at Edward as Little Bear gently settled his son on the mattress. He latched the tailgate and only then turned to look at Edward.

"I am Little Bear," he said, extending his hand. Edward took the hand and returned the light grip.

"Yes," said Edward. "I know..."

Tony ambled out of the Hospice with the release papers in hand. He was a full head taller than Little Bear.

"Thank you for watching over my son," said Little Bear, extending the same slight grip to Tony.

"My pleasure," said Tony. "You need to sign these papers,

sir. Release form. Just a formality."

Little Bear fixed his gaze somewhere down the road that led away from the Hospice.

"My daughter will sign," he said, indicating the young woman in the pickup.

"Needs to be you sir," he said. "Parent, legal guardian... You know."

"No," he said quietly. "I do not know about these things." He continued to gaze down the road, though his eyes had narrowed and the line of his jaw seemed harder. "I am not able to sign..."

"Oh..." said Tony. "It's not necessary to actually write it—your name. You can make a mark, like an X, and your daughter can sign next to it. I'll sign as a witness. That be okay?"

Little Bear turned and looked at Tony.

"It must be done?"

"Yes. The law requires it."

"The law." His shoulders sagged slightly. "...The-law. There are many strange things in the-law. Your law." He took the pen Tony offered and made his mark on the paper. Dawn signed next to it, and Tony signed as a witness.

Edward brought the Kmart bag and the box of diapers to David.

"There's a prescription in the bag," he said. "Get it filled when you get home. You've got enough meds with you for at least a week. You be home by then?"

"Be home tomorrow" said David, "the way Papa drives."

"You gonna be comfortable?" said Edward. "I mean back here?"

"I grew up in the back of a pickup," he said. "All Indian kids do."

Little Bear walked around the rear of the truck on his way to the cab.

"This is my son," he said.

"Yes," said Edward.

110

"He is a fine son." There was a fierceness in his tone. "A fine son."

"I know," said Edward.

Little Bear opened the cab door, started the truck, slammed the door closed and was off without another word. David propped himself up on one elbow and waved weakly as the truck sped away. Edward and Tony stood in the parking lot and waved until the pickup was out of sight.

"I hope he makes it home," said Tony.

"Isn't that where they're headed?"

"I mean alive."

"...Oh."

He will, said Sarah. I didn't go through all this trouble to have him die on the way.

And did he learn. . .what he was supposed to learn? said Edward.

Most of it. Hardly anybody gets it all in one lifetime. Practice, practice, practice.

God. . .You just keep coming back til you get it right? That it? Didn't I read that somewhere?

It's actually a little more complicated, said Sarah, but that's close enough for now.

CHAPTER 14

He was walking by Mr. Hall's room when he heard Sarah's voice.

. . .Go in and ask him about the car wreck, she said.
. . .What car wreck?
Just ask him. I'll explain later.

He left the Cocktail Cart outside and strolled into the room. Mr. Hall was staring at the ceiling.
"Afternoon, Mr. Hall," said Edward.
Mr. Hall didn't respond.
"Something off the Cocktail Cart today?"
He closed his eyes for a second, but didn't speak.

. . .The car wreck, said Sarah.
I know, I know, said Edward.

"You want to talk about that car wreck?" said Edward.
Mr. Hall looked out the window for a moment before he

spoke.

"What do you know about a car wreck?" he said.

. . . You heard him talking in his sleep, said Sarah.

"You were talking in your sleep awhile back. Something about a car wreck. I just wondered."

. . . Outside Bakersfield. On the Grapevine.

"Outside Bakersfield?" said Edward. "On the Grapevine?"
"God," said Mr. Hall, shaking his head. "The car wreck... God Awmighty. Nineteen and thirty six it was, but I can still see it like it was right here." He held his hand in front of his face. "Comin' out of Bakersfield in that old Ford Model A. We was godawful drunk. All of us. Rainin' cats and dogs that night. I musta had a fifth of Old Crow myself. Comin' down the L.A. side, car started goin' sideways...just spinnin' down the road till it hit a car comin' up the hill. I got tossed out and woke up in a ditch. My two buddies wasn't so lucky. Jake and Arnie Pine. One of 'em was married and had a baby boy. I never remember which one."

"Long time ago," said Edward.
"Not so long I can't remember."

. . . Sixty years and that's what he remembers, said Sarah.
So how do you not remember?, said Edward. I mean something like that? How do you forget?
I just love it when you ask questions.

"Jake and Arnie," said Mr. Hall. "God Awmighty."

. . . First thing you do is get the memory out in the open so you can see it, said Sarah. And so others can see it. That's very important, the others part. Don't you people in recovery have a

113

step that covers that? Something about admitting to God, to yourselves and to someone else the nature of your wrongs?

Yeah. Step five. The exact nature of your wrongs. Our wrongs.

Good. So that's how you start. You say-the-words. Out loud. To another person. Get it from inside to outside. Inside it's dark. Things grow in there—mushrooms, toads, bad memories. That's what those therapy people do; they go in with flashlights and look in all the dark corners. At least that's what the good ones do. So eventually you forget the original incident, you bury it so deep that you can't find it, and what you're left with is the overwhelming sense that something is terribly wrong, that you're basically a defective person and nothing is ever going to work out. Ever...

Well, wiping out your two best friends in a car accident while you're drunk is probably not going to win you any Good Citizen awards.

Granted, said Sarah. And a certain amount of remorse is appropriate. But not sixty years. After awhile people use those things as excuses. Not very healthy. So the lesson is?..Edward?

...Don't drive drunk?

That's advice, said Sarah. Not a lesson.

Give me a hint.

We're talking about forgiveness, Edward—a very important part of the process. One of the most powerful tools available at Level One. That and gratitude. And of course forgiveness includes self-forgiveness.

"Went to school with them boys," said Mr. Hall.

"...Nice guys?" said Edward.

"Wasn't for me they'd still be alive."

...What if he doesn't get it? said Edward. The lesson. Maybe not in time.

There's always next time.

114

There is?

Edward. . .some of this doesn't translate very well, so you'll have to accept it on faith. You see, time doesn't really exist—not outside Level One. It's very hard to explain because you don't have a vocabulary for it. You know the part about, You just keep coming back till you get it right?

Yeah.

That's true as far as it goes, but it just doesn't go very far. You understand?

No.

Okay, said Sarah. We'll leave it at that. You just keep coming back till you get it right. That'll do for now.

But how. . .

"Wish I'd got killed instead of them," said Mr. Hall.

"You do?"

"Honest to God I do."

". . .Why?"

Mr. Hall gave him a quick sideways glance.

"Don't take no Einstein to figure out how bad it was after that. How bad I felt about it."

"And you felt you were responsible?"

"I was the driver," he said. "Who else?"

Maybe the other driver had a flat tire and swerved into your lane.

"What if the other car had a flat tire and swerved into your lane?" said Edward.

"Didn't happen that way."

"You sure? You said you were drinking. You remember everything?"

". . .Enough."

Mr. Hall eyed him suspiciously.

"How come you think you know so much, young fella?"

115

"Oh…Some things just come to me."

"That so? You know so much, what's my middle name?"

Graham, said Sarah

"…Graham."

"Too easy. That'd be in my records. What's my first wife's name?…and what did I call her?"

"…Martha was her real name," said Edward, "and you called her Cookie."

. . .Where'd that come from? said Edward.
. . .Beats me, said Sarah.

Mr. Hall closed his eyes and took a deep breath.

"Don't that beat all," he said.

"You believe in God?" said Edward.

I can't believe you just said that, said Sarah. You the same guy who said he wasn't sure about the whole God thing?

"I been a Christian mostly. Tried the best I know how."

"You think God forgives people?"

Mr. Hall paused for a moment before he answered.

"…I believe He does. Leastways He can. You know God don't go easy on everybody."

"No?…Why is that?"

"…Just don't."

Mr. Hall crinkled the bedsheet with the bony fingers of his left hand.

"You s'pose it's true?" he said.

"About what?"

"About that other car havin' a flat tire and all. Swervin' into my lane."

"Could be," said Edward. "Otherwise they'd have thrown

116

you in jail. I mean if it was your fault and you were drunk. You didn't go to jail?"

"No...Don't that beat all," he said, shaking his head. "Mighta been just what happened."

"Mighta been," said Edward.

Mr. Hall tried to push himself up in bed. "So you was a ballplayer, eh? Pitcher?"

"Yeah. How'd you know I was a pitcher?"

"Oh," said Mr. Hall. "It just kinda come to me. You know how it is." A faint smile pulled at the corner of his mouth. "I figured a long, lanky kid like you was probably a thrower... You ever make it to the Bigs?"

"No, just minor league. Had a million dollar arm and a two bit brain." He tapped his temple. "No sense. Fell in love with a whiskey bottle early on."

"Huh. Bet you wasn't the first one," said Mr. Hall. "Or the last. I've knowed a few myself...How about helpin' me into my wheelchair and takin' me out for a smoke?"

Edward was in the habit of checking medical records before he went on his rounds and he knew that Mr. Hall was suffering from terminal lung cancer that had recently metastasized to the brain. He looked at Mr. Hall as if he had not heard the question correctly.

"The wheelchair," Mr. Hall said impatiently. "Outside the door. You can't help I'll get someone else."

Edward retrieved the wheelchair and pushed it next to the bed.

"Too late to quit smokin'," said Mr. Hall, anticipating the question. "Way too late. Besides, a man my age don't have much left. Me? I like a smoke and a whiskey sometimes. You got any whiskey on that cart?"

"I do."

"Good. You smoke?"

"No."

"Just as well...You drink?"

117

"Not any more."

"What'a you do to keep the cobwebs off?"

"I...I'm married," said Edward.

"That excitin'?"

"...Sometimes."

"Don't that beat all," said Mr. Hall. "I never had no excitin' marriages."

Edward lowered the railing on the side of the bed.

Mr. Hall removed the oxygen tubes from his nose and struggled to a sitting position.

"I can do without the air for awhile," he said. "I ain't that bad off."

"Okay."

"You ever hear of Carl Hubbell?" said Mr. Hall.

"Sure," said Edward. "King Carl."

"That's him. I played with him. On the Giants...The Dodgers were horseshit even then. Always been...If you hurry, we can watch Wheel of Fortune. You ever see it?"

"I have."

"Some show, eh?"

"Yeah, some show."

Supporting Mr. Hall's upper body, Edward eased him around and gently lowered him into the wheelchair.

"Don't forget my...bag," said Mr. Hall, pointing to the transparent catheter bag hanging from the bedframe.

"Okay," said Edward, trying to remember what they told him about catheter bags when he was in training.

"That's some show," said Mr. Hall. "That Wheel of Fortune? I could make money on that show. Maybe win a car. Somethin'...Don't take no Einstein to figure out a puzzle."

Edward unhooked the bag from the bed railing and hooked it under the wheelchair.

"Fasten you seatbelts," he said. "We're off to the races."

"...Put her in high gear and let her rip, young fella."

118

CHAPTER 15

Bea Toller, the Director of Volunteers, loved a good Trivial Pursuit game. (That and Bingo were the most popular patient activities). Whenever there were enough patients capable of playing, she herded them all down to the Family Room for a game. Great therapy, she always said. Keeps the mind working. Some had developed specialties. Miss Gladys was considered the expert on religious questions. Mr. Ambrose was always forthcoming, if not always accurate, on questions about old movies and big bands. For all her denial about not knowing anything about science (Oh, Roger would surely know the answer), Mrs. Watkins knew a good deal more than she let on. Eldon was good on flowers. Mr. Barnett covered the jazz and blues scene while Mrs. Mathews was better on things contemporary. When Mr. Hall made one of his rare appearances, he covered the world of sports. Mrs. McKelvey (who loved Bingo best, but tried to be tolerant of the Trivial Pursuit crowd) knew a little history, and Mrs. Reardon was there mostly to lend a cynical air to the proceedings. (Nobody gives a rat's ass, she'd say. We'll all be dead soon anyway.)

Bea, a substantial woman of boundless energy, usually read the questions and kept score. (But we're not dead *now*, is what she'd say to Mrs. Reardon. And now is all we have. So let the game begin...her arm raised in a gesture similar to a black power salute.)

"Did you hear that The Baby died?" Mrs. McKelvey whispered to Mrs. Mathews one Friday when they had gathered for a Game.

"Oh, no," said Mrs. Mathews, tears already forming in her eyes. "The Baby?"

"Yes."

Mrs. Mathews stared at the coffee table for a few minutes before she looked up.

"I don't know who The Baby is..." She put her hand to her mouth. "Oh, my God."

"Baby Rachelle?" said Mrs. McKelvey. "Little black baby in the Nursery? Pretty white ribbons in her hair. We'd call her a pickaninny in my day."

"...Oh," said Mrs. Mathews.

"Spina buffalo," said Mr. Ambrose, leaning on his walker.

"Spina buffalo?" said Mrs. McKelvey. "What in the world is Spina buffalo?"

"S'what she had," he said. "Somethin' like that."

"Spina bifida," said Mrs. Muggeridge, thin as a shadow, barely causing a ripple on the couch where she was sitting. "My grandson had it...something to do with the spine."

"I thought she died of a respiratory disease," said Mrs. McKelvey.

"Prob'ly did," said Mr. Ambrose. "How good can you breathe if your spine don't work right."

They turned to Mrs. Toller for clarification. She had a round face and curly red hair like Orphan Annie.

"It's true," she said. "Baby Rachelle died this morning. Some kind of breathing problem. You remember they always had that vaporizer going in her room."

Mrs. Mathews burst into tears.

"Oh, The Baby," she said. "How sad. I was going to send her a Valentine card. With little hearts and everything. Is Valentine's Day soon?"

"Fairly soon," said Mrs. Toller. "First there's Thanksgiving, then Christmas and then it's a little while later."

"I'm going to get everyone a Valentine card," said Mrs. Mathews, clapping her hands. "Everybody..." She began to sing My Funny Valentine through the tears.

Mr. Barnett smiled, thinking back to the fifties and sixties when Gerry Mulligan and Chet Baker did it at Newport—My Funny Valentine. He put the voice simulator to his throat and hummed along; he sounded like an electric razor.

Mrs. Toller tapped the coffee table with the Trivial Pursuit cards to get everyone's attention.

"Everybody ready? First question...Who wrote The Grapes of Wrath?"

Mr. Ambrose cackled noisily in anticipation of getting the first answer.

"Henry Fonder," he said triumphantly.

All eyes were on Mrs. Toller for confirmation.

"...That's close, Mr. Ambrose, but not quite it."

"What'a you mean?" he said. "I seen that movie a dozen times."

"That's who was in the movie," she said. "Henry Fonda. We're looking for who wrote the book."

"Oh, the book," said Mr. Ambrose, thumping his walker a few times for emphasis. "Whyn't you say so? I don't have no idea who wrote the book. I didn't even know there *was* a book."

"...Maybe we can give you partial credit," said Mrs. Toller. "Say two points, for knowing about the movie and all."

There was a general disapproving grumble at the suggestion, though no one actually said anything.

"…I don't want no favors," said Mr. Ambrose, when it was apparent no one was going to approve.

"God bless The Baby," said Mrs. Mathews, still sobbing. "I was a mother once…How could she just die like that?"

"If you ask me," said Mrs. Muggeridge, "it was probably food poisoning. Absolutely criminal the things they feed us around here."

"Is the food bad?" said Mrs. Mathews.

"Hemingway?" said Mrs. McKelvey.

Mrs. Toller shook her head.

"Now there was a guy who could drink," said Mrs. Reardon. "He probably had vodka for breakfast, too. Him and Catherine the Great. Vodka and Wheaties, the breakfast of champions. He was smart, though…he blew his brains out before they could put him in a place like this."

"Steinbeck?" said Eldon.

"Very good," said Mrs. Toller. "Five points for Eldon."

"What was The Baby's name?" said Mrs. Mathews.

"…Rachelle."

Mr Ambrose coughed loudly to indicate his presence.

"And no points for Mr. Ambrose," said Mrs. Reardon. She turned and stared at him with those forget-me-not eyes. "Rules are rules," she said sweetly.

"Huh," said Mr. Ambrose. "What do I care about points."

"I'm going to send Baby Rachelle a Valentine card," Mrs. Mathews announced. "I had babies once…" She closed her eyes for a moment. "But I can't remember where they are."

"That'll be nice," said Mrs. Toller. "Just give the card to me and I'll mail it for you."

"Praise Jesus," said Miss Gladys. "Baby Rachelle be home in the arms of Jesus now."

"Get the address," said Mrs. Reardon. "Mrs. Mathews wants to send her a card."

"Next question," said Mrs. Toller. "According to the Bible, what was God's first act of creation?"

122

Mrs. Mathews leaned sideways in her wheelchair and threw up on the floor. Mrs. Toller got up quickly and headed for the door.

"Don't worry," she said. "I'll get housekeeping."

"Roger would know what to do," said Mrs. Watkins, looking the other way. "He'd snap his fingers and it'd get done."

"You ought to do that in your room," said Mrs. McKelvey. "In the toilet."

Mrs. Mathews looked mystified.

"Do what?" she said.

"Praise Jesus," said Miss Gladys.

"What you just did," said Mrs. McKelvery.

"...Did I do something wrong?"

The lady from Housekeeping arrived moments later and had it cleaned up in a few seconds, her gloved hands and big sponge a blur of motion. Mercy Mendez was a housekeeping whiz; people throwing up on the floor was business as usual for her.

"Okay," said Mrs. Toller, resuming her position at the head of the table. "Where were we?"

"We be talkin' 'bout God," said Miss Gladys.

"Right...The question was—According to the Bible, what was God's first act of creation?"

"Sickness most likely," said Mrs. Reardon. "Cancer... Seems to be more of that than anything else."

Mr. Barnett placed the simulator to the side of his neck and spoke into a lull in the conversation.

"God-made-the-blues," he said in his buzzy montone, chuckling silently.

"...The what?" said Mrs. McKelvey.

"Adam and Eve?" said Mrs. Reardon.

"No."

"Scotch and soda?"

"No."

"Pumpkins?" said Eldon.

"Everything," said Mrs. Watkins. "Regardless of what Roger thought, I've always been a believer. Deep down. I know that God made everything."

"Could God make a rock so heavy He couldn't lift it?" said Mr. Ambrose. "That's a primary question."

"When I say my prayers tonight," said Mrs. Mathews. "I'm going to pray to The Baby because she's in heaven now. I always heard that…That little babies go straight to heaven because they've never done anything wrong. You think that's true, Mrs. Toller?"

"I can't imagine why not," said Mrs. Toller.

"…Why not what?" said Mrs. Mathews.

"Why she wouldn't be in heaven."

"…Why who wouldn't be in heaven?"

"Next time you feel like you're going to be sick," said Mrs. Toller, "try to remember to use the bag you have."

Mrs. Mathews picked up the bag and waved it.

"Oh, I will," she said brightly. "It's very handy. I always keep it with me. Just in case."

"You see," said Mr. Ambrose, "if God could make a rock so heavy He couldn't lift it, that means He can't do everything. He's not all powerful like they say."

"Praise Jesus," said Miss Gladys.

"Well, first of all," said Mrs. Watkins, "that's not even a real question. Not a valid one. It contains a…double negative. At least one. It's a contradiction in terms."

"It's just a question," said Mr. Ambrose. "Yes or no."

Edward arrived for his shift and stood at the back of the room with Mary Blanchard and Big Tony. Mrs. Reardon spotted him the minute he walked in.

"Cocktail time?" she said.

"Almost," he said, glancing at his watch.

"Don't be late," she said. "I don't have all day."

"I know…I won't be late."

Miss Gladys held up both hands, palms open; even with her arms up you could barely see her sitting in the corner of the couch. She was wearing her I Have A Dream button from her civil rights days when she marched with King in Selma and later in the March on Washington. She had recently been giving away her personal belongings, as if she knew she would be leaving soon.

"In the beginnin'," she said, "God created heaven and earth...That's the first thing in the Bible."

"Very good, Miss Gladys," said Mrs. Toller. "Five points for you."

"Then He made the light, and then He. . ."

"Bud Light?" said Mrs. Reardon.

Miss Gladys frowned but did not reply.

"When did the pumpkins come?" said Eldon.

She considered that for a moment.

"The third day He make the seas and the lands and all the vegetations."

"So pumpkins were here before man, eh?"

"Praise Jesus," said Miss Gladys. "The Lord God Hisself made man on the sixth day and He look all around and say, *It be very good.*"

"When'd He create cancer?" said Mrs. Reardon. "...Right after He made man? So people would have something to pray about?"

Mr. Hall sat quietly in his wheelchair, staring at a spot somewhere above Mrs. Toller's head.

"I was in a terrible accident once," he said. "Car swerved into my lane and hit me. Hit my car...Killed my two best friends. Throwd 'em clean outta the car."

"...I'm sorry to hear that," said Mrs. Toller. "It was a long time ago? The accident?"

"Yep. Long time ago."

"About the time God was making man in His own image," said Mrs. Reardon.

"Praise Jesus…"

"So…" said Mrs. Toller. "Miss Gladys and Eldon are tied with five points each. Here's the next question…Who was the last Triple Crown winner?"

"Seabiscuit," said Mr. Ambrose. "Hands down. Best horse ever wore a saddle."

"This is a person, I believe," said Mrs. Toller.

"Man-o-war?" said Mr. Ambrose.

"Let me read the question again," said Mrs. Toller. "Who was baseball's last Triple Crown winner?"

"Oh, baseball," said Mr. Ambrose. "Whyn't you say so?"

"What's a Triple Crown?" said Mrs. Watkins.

"Average, home runs and RBI's," said Mr. Hall.

"Oh…" said Mrs. Watkins. She leaned over toward Mrs. Muggeridge. "What'd he say?" she whispered.

"Just some gobbledegook," said Mrs. Muggeridge.

"And on the seventh day," said Mrs. Reardon, "God created Triple Crown vodka. You'll never frown with Triple Crown. They sell it at all the best Thrifty Drug Stores. Takes your goddam breath away…"

"Joltin' Joe Dimaggio," said Mr. Ambrose.

"No," said Mrs. Toller.

"Kermit the Frog," said Eldon.

"…Carl Yastremski," said Mr. Hall. "Nineteen and sixty-seven."

"Oh, very good," said Mrs. Toller.

"You mean it really was Kermit?" said Eldon.

"No," said Mrs. Toller. "It was Carl Yastremski."

"It wasn't Joe Dimaggio?" said Mr. Ambrose.

"No."

"Huh. Maybe he won the Preakness. Or the Belmost."

"…Ready for the next question?" said Mrs. Toller.

"I got a little brain fever today," said Mr. Ambrose. "I'm not as mental as I usually am."

"That's very understandable," said Mrs. Toller.

126

"Before that it was Frank Robinson," said Mr. Hall. "Then you gotta go back ten years to Mickey Mantle."

"The next question," said Mrs. Toller. "Who invented the steamboat?"

"You got no music questions?" said Mr. Ambrose. "Big Band stuff. Or movies. I'm good at movies. I'm the best."

"Oh, I know," said Mrs. McKelvey. "It was Eli Whitney."

"Oh, that's very close," Mrs. Toller said gently. "But I think Eli Whitney was associated with the cotton gin."

"What kind of gin?" said Mrs. Reardon.

"Could you repeat the question?" said Mrs. Mathews.

"Of course…Who invented the steamboat?"

"I wanted to join the circus when I was young," said Eldon.

"Well," said Mrs. Reardon. "It took awhile but here you are. If this isn't a circus, I don't know what is."

"Did someone just throw up?" said Mrs. Mathews. "It smells like that."

Mrs. McKelvey put a hand on her forearm.

"You did, dearie," she said.

"…Who did?"

"You did."

"…Oh," said Mrs. Mathews. "Imagine that."

"Before that it was Ted Williams maybe," said Mr. Hall. "Teddy ballgame. Nineteen and…forty-seven I believe it was."

"I had a cousin named Teddy," said Mrs. Muggeridge. "My brother Ernie's boy. Never did a thing but cause his daddy grief."

"It was Robert Fulton who invented the steamboat," Mrs. Mathews said quietly. "First one launched in France, eighteen oh three. First commericial one in the United States in eighteen oh seven."

A full twenty seconds of silence followed the answer. She sat smiling serenely, gazing into space, while everyone looked on. She seemed not to notice.

Where did all that come from? said Edward.

Oh, it's just information, Sarah said casually. It's available to everyone.

It is? Then how come everyone's not able to come up with Robert Fulton and France, eighteen oh three, and New York, eighteen oh seven?

Because, Edward, you've been taught that the information is inaccessible.

That's it? That's all that's keeping us from getting it?

That's all, said Sarah. It's so simple that everyone misses it.

So Mrs. Mathews just tunes in and gets it?

Yes. Pity is, it's more a function of brain cancer than belief for our Mrs. Mathews.

"...That's very good, Mrs. Mathews," said Mrs. Toller. "Amazing, actually. Such a wealth of information. We really ought to give you five more points for extra credit."

"Oh, there's Uncle Dan," said Mrs. Mathews, pointing excitedly across the room. "And The Baby. Oh, goodness, look at them all."

Mr. Ambrose coughed and thumped his walker a few times.

"Rules is rules," he said. "Right answers is five points only. No extras available at this store. You got any movie questions? I'm great on movies. I seen most every movie ever made."

Mrs. Toller looked at the next few cards.

"Here's one," she said "...Who played Richard Blaine in Casablanca?"

"Hah!" said Mr. Ambrose. "That's easy. It was..."

"Humphrey Bogart," Mrs. Mathews said quickly. "Also starring Ingrid Bergman, Peter Lorre, Sydney Greenstreet..."

"I'm having some trouble here," said Mr. Ambrose. "I was giving the answer to that question when this lady interrupted with..."

"...Claude Rains, Dooley Wilson, Cuddles Sakall, Paul Henreid." She touched her temples with her fingers. "Oh, my...My oh my...What a headache." Her head suddenly sank to her chest as she went limp and almost fell out of the wheelchair.

Tony moved forward quickly, turned the wheelchair around and wheeled her out of the room.

No one spoke for awhile. Then Mrs. Toller:

"Well, I think we can give Mr. Ambrose some credit for a correct answer...On the Casablanca question. After all, he did know the answer. Mrs. Mathews was certainly accurate and thorough, but I think it's only fair that we recognize Mr. Ambrose's efforts."

Mr. Ambrose stared hard at the crossbar on his new chrome walker.

"You know, Mrs....Matty" he said slowly. "It wasn't such a big thing, you bein' sick on my walker that time. Heck, it wiped right off. Clean as a whistle. Good as new almost. You know me. I'm very excitable sometimes. But I didn't mean to cause you no sorrow about it."

...And what would the lesson be here? said Sarah.
Don't wait?
Explain...
Don't wait to say you're sorry, to say I love you. Say it now. All of it. Do it now. Tomorrow may be too late. The next few minutes may be too late.
Good. Mrs. Reardon is right, of course. She doesn't have all day. Nobody does. All we have is now. So do it now. Be it now. Don't wait...Laugh now. Cry now. Love now. Forgive now. Be forgiven now. Make the phone call you've been meaning to make. If you're waiting to get better, or for it to get better, you can stop waiting because you, or it, will never be any better than it is right now. Tomorrow will just be different.

Another day with a different date. There is no better; there is only now.

The room was silent in the absence of Mrs. Mathews—the only sounds were the labored breathing of the occupants. Mrs. Toller shuffled aimlessly through the Trivial Pursuit cards. Mr. Ambrose shifted his walker. Eldon stared at his Kermit-the-Frog slippers.

"...Praise Jesus," Miss Gladys said finally. "That lady gone home to the Lo'd. Praise be..."

"Matter of fact," said Mr. Hall, "I think Ted Williams won it before that, too."

"Do you suppose she's...gone?" said Mrs. Watkins.

"A rose by any other name," said Mrs. Reardon. "What do you think, Mrs. Toller? You think she's kicked the bucket, or just temporarily gone out of action?"

"I think we'd better wait for official word," said Mrs. Toller. "No use speculating. She may just have a terrible headache. She's had those before."

"Who was she talking to?" said Mrs. Watkins. "Did you hear? Didn't she say something about Uncle Dan...and The Baby?"

Mr. Barnett began to sing in his metallic monotone:

"...Pack-up-all-your-cares-and-woes-here-I-go-singin'-low...bye-bye -blackbird."

"Probably food poisoning," said Mrs. Muggeridge.

Mrs. Watkins leafed through the Book of Psalms.

"...Surely goodness and mercy shall follow me all the days of my life and I shall dwell in the house of the Lord forever."

"Amen," said Miss Gladys.

"The Great Pumpkin rides across the night sky," Eldon said softly, "bringing toys to all the little boys and girls. Hello, Great Pumpkin...We love you."

Mary Blanchard broke the awkward silence that began to settle in the room.

130

"I don't know about you, but I'm done wore out for the day," she said. "Let's call it quits and send the Cocktail Man around before dinner."

"Hurray," said Mrs. Reardon.

"Ugh," said Mrs. Muggeridge. "Dinner."

The somber procession of wheelchairs left the Family Room in silence. Only Mr. Hall seemed occupied with thoughts other than Mrs. Mathews.

"...But who was before Ted Williams?" he wondered.

CHAPTER 16

"Are you a religious person?" said Mrs. Watkins.

"Oh, I don't think I'd call myself a religious person," said Edward.

"But you believe in God?"

"...I believe in some Power that I think is keeping track of things. That I hope is keeping track of things."

"Were you brought up in a religious home?" said Mrs. Watkins.

"I think so," said Edward. "We were very Catholic."

"My family were Methodists, though I never told Roger. He had a strong aversion to Methodists. And Catholics, and Lutherans and all the rest."

"We were...maybe what you could call traditional Catholics. We had fish every Friday, went to Mass every Sunday and had fights almost every night. We were known in the neighborhood as the Fighting Gallaghers."

"Oh, my," said Mrs. Watkins. "That must have been awful."

"It wasn't so bad. Mostly because I didn't find out till later that everyone's house wasn't like that. You just think it's normal—people and furniture flying across the room, dishes breaking, an occasional gunshot, just another night at the Gallaghers."

"Oh, my…"

"But that's old news, Mrs. Watkins," said Edward. "Let's talk about something more important. Have you done the poem we talked about last week? The one you promised me?"

"I haven't done a big epic, Edward. And it's not finished, mind you. But I did one, at least started one. It's about Bingo players trying to get into heaven."

"Great," said Edward.

Mrs. Watkins sat quietly for a moment, the poem in her hand.

"…Did you know, Edward, that after God sent all those trials and tribulations to Job, He ended up giving him twice as much as he had before. Imagine—twice as much. As a reward. Isn't that amazing?"

"And as I recall, Job had a lot to start with."

"Oh, yes. He had land and sheep and camels and oxen. Children. Just everything."

"And why did God take all that stuff away? I can never remember that part."

"It was to test him," said Mrs. Watkins. "You see, the Devil tells God that Job worships Him just because he has all these…material things. The camels and oxen and such. And if they were taken away, the Devil says that Job would curse God. So that's why God takes everything away. To test him. And to prove to the Devil that Job is a good man."

"You think Job felt like some kind of a pawn in this cosmic chess game between the Devil and God?"

"Oh, no," said Mrs. Watkins. "I think he was a true believer who knew that in the end God would reward him. He never wavered."

"I'm afraid I'm not such a great believer," said Edward.

"I'm more like the reed blowing in the wind. Not a good candidate for unwavering faith. I knew a prison chaplain once who said that doubt was a normal part of the process."

"...A prison chaplain?" said Mrs. Watkins.

"Did I say prison chaplain?"

"I think so..."

"I meant ex-prison chaplain," said Edward. "He was at-one-time a prison chaplain. Years ago. At least that's what he said. You ever go to Our Lady of Sorrows?"

"...In Wheatridge?"

"Unhuh."

"Just off Edgemont?" said Mrs. Watkins.

"That's the one."

"I've driven by it a hundred times," she said, "but I've never gone in."

"Well, that's where he's an assistant pastor. This prison chaplain. Ex-prison chaplain."

"My..."

"I'd really like to hear your poem," said Edward.

Mrs. Watkins fumbled for her glasses, put them on and squinted at the paper in her hand, moving it closer, trying to bring it into focus. She cleared her throat:

They're calling out the numbers,
As the faithful wait to hear,
In the Big Top Bingo Parlour,
Outside the Pearly Gates.
The winners get to enter soon,
But the losers have to wait.
It takes no time at all, it seems
Till Henry's close to Bingo
And I'm only one away.
But Roger's card is empty
Not a number has he matched.
His face is gray as marble,

'Cuz he knows he'll have to wait,
In the Big Top Bingo Parlour,
Outside the Pearly Gates...

"That's all I have for now," said Mrs. Watkins.

"It's wonderful," said Edward. "And it does have a certain epic quality to it."

"You think so?"

"Certainly do...You know how it's going to end?"

"I do," said Mrs. Watkins. "But you know as a writer that I can't talk about it. That would spoil it."

"I understand."

"I'd forgotten how much fun writing can be," she said. "There's all these people you create and you get them to do anything you want." She sighed and took her glasses off. "You know, sometimes I think it's all been for nothing."

"What's all been for nothing?" said Edward.

"Oh, life...everything. All these years I've been absolutely useless. Doesn't seem like I got anything done, like I accomplished anything. Years and years...wasted."

"Let me see," said Edward. "...I know a few things you've accomplished. You're a published writer, and very early in life at that. How many of us would like to say that? You were married to, and helped, Roger on his way to the Nobel Prize. No small accomplishment. I also don't think he could have done it without you. You've met the King of Sweden and you've traveled the world. You danced in the moonlight with Henry. That was probably worth the whole trip by itself."

She motioned Edward closer to the bed.

"You know what I've never done?" she said.

Edward shook his head.

"I've never gotten drunk. Not really drunk."

"No?" said Edward. "Not even when you were young?"

"No," she said. "I was very religious when I was young. Before I met Roger. Then Roger was so...so strict about everything. Just one drink for Roger. That's all. So that was all for me, too. Roger had a mission. He discouraged everything that was..."

"That was fun?"

"Yes. Discouraged everything that was fun." She seemed to be feeling the effects of the brandy she had just finished.

"How'd you like to get drunk tonight?" said Edward.

"Oh...Tonight? Right now?"

"Right now."

"What about the One Drink Rule?"

"If you won't tell, I won't."

She clapped her hands.

"Oh, yes," she said. "I think I'll do it. Would that be okay? Would you get drunk with me?"

"Not tonight," said Edward. "Bartenders should really stay sober. Besides, I have to drive the Cocktail Cart back to the office."

    ...Good thinking, said Sarah.

"You don't think it's wrong, do you?" said Mrs. Watkins. "Getting drunk?"

"Oh, no," said Edward. "There are certainly occasions when it's absolutely the right thing to do...Like now."

"...But you don't drink?"

"I don't drink anymore. But I did...I certainly did."

"Oh, I'm going to get drunk," said Mrs. Watkins, clapping her hands again. "What shall we start with? Should we have martinis and shooters and...boxcars? I've heard of all of those. What would Fred Astaire and Ginger Rogers drink?"

"They might have a brandy or two. Maybe a martini, but definitely not a shooter or a boxcar. And since we've already started on brandy, maybe we ought to stick to that. But first let me get you the right glass. Plastic cups are not the proper thing for a classy lady at a drinking party."

He hurried out of the room and returned a few minutes later with a beautiful brandy snifter.

"Compliments of Father Tom," said Edward. "He has a wonderful collection of glasses. He'll never miss it."

He poured some brandy into the glass and handed it to Mrs. Watkins.

"First you swish it around a little," he said. He took her hand with the glass in it and made a circular motion. "Then you …sniff it. Come to think of it, that's probably why they call it a snifter. You bring it up to your nose and check the aroma…the bouquet, I think they call it."

She brought it up to her nose and inhaled.

"Smells awful," she said, making a face.

"It's something of an acquired…smell," he said. "You have to get used to it."

"This what you used to drink?" said Mrs. Watkins.

"No. I drank wine mostly."

"Oh…" She took a sip of brandy and smiled. "This is extremely good, Edward. And thank you for the proper glass. You're taking very good care of me."

"My pleasure," he said.

She took another sip and held the glass with both hands.

"Just think what I've been missing all these years."

"It's never too late," said Edward.

"I wonder," she said thoughtfully. "You know, Edward, sometimes I get very frightened."

"About what?"

"Everything," she said. "That I won't do it right. That I'll end up being a burden. That I'm already a burden."

"Not so," said Edward.

"But these people have to take care of me."

"These people *want* to take care of you, Mrs. Watkins. They got these jobs because they wanted to take care of people. It's their…vocation."

"Oh, I hope so. I'd like to think that. Here I am on my

second big brandy," she said proudly. She raised her glass, drank the rest of the brandy and handed the glass back to Edward. "If you please, Mr. Bartender, another one for the lady?"

He took his time making the next drink.

"And now Mrs. Roger Watkins is about to have another brandy," she announced. "A dandy brandy...Do you suppose it's true, Edward, about the streets of gold in heaven? About angels and clouds and harps and all? You think it's true?"

"Actually I think it's mostly..."

...It's absolutely true, said Sarah. Streets of gold. Angels. Harps. Clouds. The whole thing.

I thought you said it was just...

Not for Mrs. Watkins. Not for now. She needs streets of gold and angels at the moment. She'll find out very soon that we have something much better in store for her. But for now, let her have streets of gold and clouds and harps. And after all, there really are angels. You of all people should know that. It will be a comfort at the end of a long journey. She has done many wonderful things, this lady. Learned many things. And it's nice that you are the one to serve her those last few drinks. Especially you. Do you understand why?

...I think so.

"I'm sure of it, Mrs. Watkins," he said. "No doubt at all. Streets of gold, angels, the whole thing."

"Oh, I hope so. And heavenly choirs? I love music."

"You bet," said Edward, pouring more brandy in the snifter. "Better than the Tabernacle Choir. Lots better. We're talking angelic choirs now."

...Tra la la la la, said Sarah.

Really, said Edward.

You don't think I can sing? I really was *in the heavenly choir. The real one. . . .*

"I used to sing in the choir," said Mrs. Watkins. "At Montview Methodist when I was young. I was a very good singer. Minister Tiller always remarked about what a good voice I had."

"I bet you can still sing," said Edward.

"Oh..."

She took a sip of brandy and thought about it for a moment.

"...Yes," she said finally. "I believe I can still sing."

"Would you sing something for me?"

"I only know hymns," she said. "Old hymns. Old like me."

"The old hymns are the best ones," said Edward. "Everybody knows that."

A Mighty Fortress comes to mind, said Sarah. Ask her if she remembers it.

"How about 'A Mighty Fortress'?" said Edward. "You remember that?"

"...Some of it," she said. "We used to sing it in the choir. That very song. Shall I try it?"

"Please," said Edward.

"You mean just...sing? Now?"

"Right. Just sing...What better time?"

She cleared her throat, took a deep breath and began in a shaky vibrato...

"A mighty fortress is our God, a bulwark ne-ver fail-ing." Her voice was frail but true. "A helper he amid the flood of..."

At that moment a booming baritone joined her frail soprano.

"...of mortal ills pre-vail-ing."

It was Tony, smiling broadly from the doorway.

"Ve-ry good, Mrs. Watkins," he said. "Let's start from the

139

beginning."

He raised his arms and began on the downbeat.

"A mighty fortress is our God, a bulwark ne-ver fail-ing…"

Tony knew all three verses. Mrs. Watkins followed along, smiling broadly, her voice getting stronger, tears running down her cheeks. Edward only hummed, not knowing the words, fighting back tears of his own for reasons he didn't understand. When they finished, Tony gave Mrs. Watkins a hug and a kiss and left the room. Mrs. Watkins seemed exhausted.

"Oh, my," she said. "Wasn't that something? Singing like that? You know what they say—he who sings prays twice."

She finished the brandy and let the glass slip out of her hand onto the bed.

"Dandy brandy," she said sleepily. "I think I have had quite enough to drink for now. I shall finish my poem later. And I'll break my rule about telling how it ends just this once. Want to hear?"

"Of course."

"It ends with Roger going to Hell," she said, giggling at the thought. "He spends so much time trying to get a winner at the Big Top Bingo Parlour and being so obnoxious about it, they finally send him to Hell. Just because. Isn't that awful?" Though her smile didn't indicate that she thought it was awful at all.

"No," said Edward. "It seems altogether fitting."

"Oh, my," said Mrs. Watkins. "I think I'm actually very drunk. What do you think, Edward? Am I really drunk?"

"I would say that you're very very drunk, enormously drunk, but holding your liquor like a true lady."

"How nice." Her head fell back on the pillow. "Maybe just a little nap before dinner." She closed her eyes.

…*Kiss her goodbye, said Sarah. This will be her final sleep.*

140

You mean she's. . .going?
Very soon. She won't awaken.
God, said Edward. You think the brandy brought it on?
Yes.
Then why did you let me do that? Give her all those drinks?
She wanted one last fling. One last earth experience she hadn't had before. And you helped her realize that. It was your parting gift to her.
But it probably killed her. At least helped.
True, said Sarah. But the object isn't to live forever, Edward. At least not on the earth plane. The object, if you can call it that, is simply to live until you die. That's what Mrs. Watkins did. . .So blessed be the name of Mrs. Irma Watkins. Hallelujah. . .

Edward kissed the top of her head and rested his hand on her cheek for just a moment. He thought he saw her smile, but dismissed the notion almost immediately. He blew his nose and pushed the Cocktail Cart toward the door, humming softly. . .A mighty fortress is our God, a bulwark ne-ver fail-ing. . .

CHAPTER 17

Mrs. Reardon was sitting on her bed staring out the window when he pushed the Cocktail Cart into her room the following Friday. She didn't even acknowledge his presence until he cleared his throat and rattled the bottles on the Cart. And when she did turn, her face was blank, as if she didn't know who he was. Only slowly did her expression become one of recognition—a wry smile that turned up a corner of her mouth, eyebrows raised ever so slightly.

"...Daddy," she said. "What brings you here on such a fine day?"

...That's your cue, said Sarah
Cue for what? said Edward. I have no idea what you're talking about.
Then ask for help.
...Ask who?
Just ask, said Sarah. Somebody is always listening.
Okay, here goes...Help. I need help.
The silence that followed seemed to stretch into minutes.

. . .Nobody answered, said Edward.

Actually, Somebody did answer, said Sarah. Your job now is to act-as-if you've received the information.

But I didn't hear anything.

I know. But that doesn't mean there wasn't an answer. . . necessarily.

You have no idea how confusing that sounds, said Edward.

It will help if you stop trying to make sense of it. Stop trying to be logical.

So what do I do? said Edward.

Listen with your heart, said Sarah. What does your heart say?

. . .Yo, Heart. What should we do?

Very funny, said Sarah. You may note that you heard a celestial chuckle.

. . .I give up, said Edward.

Action is the magic word, said Sarah. If you keep moving the scenery changes. If not, nothing changes. Nothing happens. And this is just a suggestion, but whatever seems right probably is right. . .

. . .Well, seems like I ought to say something.

Bravo, said Sarah. Do it. . .

Edward closed his eyes and took three deep breaths.

"I wanted to come visit," he said. "See how you were. Your mother tells me you've been feeling poorly."

"Come sit," said Mrs. Reardon, patting the bed.

Edward sat next to her.

"It's true," she said, touching her temples with her fingertips. "The headaches are back. You remember the headaches, Daddy? How I used to scream and carry on?" She rocked back and forth on the bed.

"I remember," he said.

"You used to call me Little Mary Sunshine then," she said.

"Yes. My Little Mary Sunshine."

"There were the clouds. Big dark clouds." She returned her gaze to the window. "I didn't see the sun for a long time."

"I know," he said. "I've come to ask you to forgive me. I did some terrible things."

"Did you, Daddy?"

"...Don't you remember?" said Edward.

"I remember some things. Not many...There were the clouds. I remember those."

She patted his hand.

"You should tell me, Daddy, about the things you did," she said. "Tell me so I can forgive you."

Edward closed his eyes for a moment.

"I...took advantage of you when you were very young," he said, wondering where the flood of memories was coming from. "I harmed you...molested you."

She looked at him with those big, Bambi eyes that always seemed to be full of tears that never fell, so deep there was no bottom to them. He had to look away.

"Was that you, Daddy? All those years ago?...Did I know it was you?"

She looked out the window for a long time before she continued.

"...I remember," she said slowly. "You grunted like a pig and you smelled bad...Was that you, Daddy?"

He could not bring himself to speak.

"And I remember the part about the secret," she said. "That we shared a secret, and if I ever told anyone there would be serious con-se-quen-ces. I even remember the way you said it— con-se-quen-ces. It might even kill Mommy, you said. I was going to be a Good Little Girl because I Never Told Secrets. Daddy's Good Little Girl...I liked being your Good Little Girl, Daddy. And it was fun having secrets, too. I only told one other person. Just one. Father Franklin, and he didn't believe me. Told me I should ask God to forgive me for telling such a terrible lie. I didn't even tell old Elmer Fuddy Duddy. Anyway,

144

all he could do was stand around and watch."

"...It was me, Sunshine," said Edward, aware that he was now someone with painful memories as a child molester.

"Was it really?" she said.

"...Yes."

She turned and started to pound on his chest with her tiny fists, slowly at first, then faster and faster, her frail arms like pistons, pummeling him as hard as she could. He sat and let her hit him until she was exhausted.

"No no no," she sobbed.

He put his arm around her and pulled her close.

"Oh God," she said. "...Oh God."

"I'm sorry."

"Sorry...Sorry's just a word."

He nodded.

"You broke my heart, Daddy. You know that?"

"I know," he said. "I know."

"No, you don't know, Daddy. Nobody does. You have to say you're sorry and really mean it...You have to say it now."

"...I am sorry and I *do* mean it."

"Swear on your mother's grave."

"I swear on my mother's grave," he said.

"...Did you love your mother? It only counts if you loved her."

"Yes. Very much."

She thought about it for a few moments.

"Did I ever meet her?" she said.

"You were very young when she died. Only a year or so."

"Did she love me?"

"She adored you," said Edward. "She wanted to see you grow up in the worst way."

"She was my grandmother?"

"Yes...She was your grandmother."

"Did you love your father?"

"...I don't think so."

"Why?" she said.

"Because...he wasn't a very lovable person, I guess."

"Neither was mine," she said sadly. "...What was your mother like? My grandmother."

"She was a big woman. Maybe two hundred pounds or more. But a very sweet, gentle lady. Good German stock, though she had a face like a Native American—high cheekbones and an Indian nose. When I was young I used to think she looked like the Indian on the Buffalo nickel. She died much too soon."

"Why did she die?" said Mrs. Reardon.

"...Why or when?"

"Why?"

"I don't know why for sure. Sometimes I think I know, but..."

People die because it's Time, said Sarah.

...What does that mean?

Unfortunately, you'll have to wait to find out. For now, try to think of it as Time To Move On...

"...I'm not sure why anyone dies," he said.

"I know why I'm going to die."

"Do you?" said Edward. "Why?"

"Because it's Time."

...See, said Sarah. She already knows.

"How do you know that?" said Edward. "Know when it's Time?"

She shrugged.

"I just do," she said.

"Can you forgive me, Sunshine?" said Edward. "For all the things I did?"

She put her index finger to her lips and thought about it.

"...I think I can," she said. "At least maybe. Can you forgive me for telling Father Franklin our secret? Even after I promised?"

"Oh, Sunshine," he said, holding her closer, "there's nothing to fogive. You didn't do anything wrong."

He rocked her in his arms for a few minutes.

"Do you ever wonder what it would have been like?" he said. "What your life would have been like if...none of that had ever happened."

She didn't speak for a long time. And when she did, she didn't acknowledge the question.

"Remember when I could run like the wind, Daddy?" she said, her voice clear and young.

"Yes."

"Before everything happened and the clouds came. All the boys were after me then—Chester and Rob and Billy and the rest. Oh, I bet I was a sight."

"You were," he said, picturing a young girl running across the yard by the old split log fence, pigtails flying. "Pretty as could be. Your mother braided your hair. Remember that?"

"She combed it first with that big black comb. Always pulled my hair too tight. Hurt like the dickens. *Ouch, Mama! Don't pull my hair out.*" She touched her hair and let her hand rest for a moment on his.

"You always had pretty hair, Sunshine."

"Pretty hair," she said dreamily. "I was the girl with the pretty hair."

"That you were."

"Such a long time ago," she said. "...Did you know Catherine the Great drank vodka for breakfast, Daddy?"

"I didn't."

"I do that now, you know—drink vodka for breakfast. My last husband just had a fit every time I did it. Robert? You remember Robert, Daddy? Little pencil moustache and a big old tummy?"

"I...I don't think so," said Edward.

"Not surprising," she said. "He wasn't around very long. He was delving into the mysteries of the East while I was having vodka for breakfast. It wasn't such a good match, anyway. But they all died, Daddy. I ever tell you that?"

"Who all died?"

"All my husbands. All six. That always seemed like a large number of husbands, but the bartender here said it wasn't out of the ordinary. At least not too far out of the ordinary. Now they're all dead and here I am."

She lowered her voice to a whisper.

"But not for long," she confided. "Before you know it we'll all be dead as doornails. They're coming in through the windows in the basement, releasing poison gas through the pipes, violating me when the lights go out. God, the things that happen here. No wonder I have vodka for breakfast."

"...No wonder," he said.

"They have a man that's supposed to be protecting us," she said. "Mr. Bill the Maintenance Man. Just one man, Daddy, against a whole army. You think that's enough?"

"Wouldn't seem like it."

"Maybe you could stay and help," she said. "We'd have a better chance with you here. And I'd just feel...safer."

"I'll be here as long as you need me, Sunshine."

"Promise?"

"Cross my heart," he said.

She leaned her head on his chest. He stroked her hair.

"Could we go to the movies, Daddy? Remember when we used to do that?"

"Yes."

"We went to just the best movies. Gone With The Wind, Goodbye Mr. Chips...Boys Town."

"...With Dick Tracy," said Edward. "That was your favorite."

"Oh, Daddy," she said. "*Spencer* Tracy. You always say

148

Dick Tracy instead of Spencer Tracy."

"That's right. I remember."

She closed her eyes for a few moments. When she opened them, she sat up, looked at Edward and blinked several times.

"Is it four o'clock yet?" she said.

"A little after," said Edward.

"Then it must be time for a drink, Mr. Bartender."

"Sounds right to me," said Edward, getting up from the bed. "The usual, Mrs. Reardon."

"The usual...You know I just had the strangest dream about my father."

"Oh?"

"Yes. My father was an actor. A movie actor. He was in Boys Town. Tracy was his name. Spencer Tracy. You may have heard of him."

"Oh, yes. So you're Spencer Tracy's little girl."

"Yes. He was very talented, my father. He drank a bit, but in other ways he was a good person. He treated me very well. Like a princess...Don't forget to put some goddam vodka in that thing. Hardly seems like anybody around here knows how to make a decent drink."

"I used to tend bar at the Zebra Room," said Edward.

"And I used to drink there," she said. "Small world, eh?"

"Yeah."

"And I was never, ever a prostitute, young man. Regardless of what people say, the only thing I ever had to sell was some furniture and that old piano that never worked anyway. You believe me?"

"Of course I do."

"...I'm going on a journey soon," she said.

"Where to?"

"To see my father. He has a place up in the mountains."

"That mean you'll be leaving us soon?"

She shrugged.

"Maybe...Maybe not. It's hard to say. I don't know if it's

Time yet."

She sat up and peered at the Cocktail Cart. "Do you have any limes, young man? For my drink? I can hardly have a drink without a slice of lime."

"I'll have to go to the kitchen and get one, Mrs. Reardon. You'll watch the Cart, won't you? Make sure nobody steals anything."

She smiled and leaned back on one elbow.

"Of course," she said. "I'm the lady who watches the Cart. Everyone knows me here. If you can't trust Mary Reardon, who can you trust."

He walked slowly to the kitchen, retrieved a lime and sauntered back to Mrs. Reardon's room. When he walked in the door, the vodka bottle was still wobbling on the cart. Mrs. Reardon was propped up on one elbow, holding a glass of clear liquid in one hand, smiling at Edward.

"Here we are," he said. "One lime for Mrs. Reardon."

"Just slice it thin and put it in a glass," she said. "I'll drink this water and you can put it in here. A little ice. Just a little. Too much and it ruins the taste of the vodka. Did you know that Catherine the Great drank vodka for breakfast? That was Catherine the Second. I have no idea what Catherine the First drank. Blood maybe. Or vodka and orange juice. You think they had oranges then? That long ago."

"Oranges have probably been around for a long time."

She drank the clear liquid and handed the glass to Edward. Her eyes were watering.

Edward made a Bloody Mary, put a twist of lime in it and set it on the tray next to the bed.

Mrs. Reardon settled back on the pillow and stared at the ceiling.

"You know," she said, "...I've been very tired lately. Exceptionally. If I should pass this way again, young man, you'll remember me, won't you?"

"I won't forget you, Mrs. Reardon," he said. "Ever..."

150

"That's good. It's nice to be remembered, to live in memory for a time. I had husbands, you know, but they're all dead."

She closed her eyes and began to breath evenly. Edward stayed for a moment, then touched her hand and quietly pushed the Cocktail Cart out into the hallway.

. . .How did all that happen?

Amazing, isn't it? said Sarah. How everything is connected. All the memories and all the experiences. You just happened to tap into another existence so she could complete her life cycle this time around.

. . .Did I become someone else? Seemed like I actually was her father for awhile.

For now, just try to think of it as all things being connected. Try to think of consciousness as strands. . .that connect everything.

What do they look like? said Edward.

I just knew you were going to ask that. The answer is. . . they don't look like anything because you can't actually see them. And even if you could, you don't have the vocabulary to describe them. So for now, just try to think of them as strands that connect everything. Strands of gold, if you like. That helps some people. . .

But why. . .

You're going to get some serious demerits, Edward, if you keep pursuing this why business. More will be revealed, Edward. Remember that? You can only know so much for now.

"Save me a seat," said Mrs. Reardon, sitting up and looking toward the foot of the bed. . ."I'll get the popcorn."

Edward turned and looked back at her. She was smiling and hugging a teddy bear to her chest. Though he had been in her room dozens of times, he had never seen a teddy bear. He shook his head and continued out of the room. In the

151

background he could hear Sarah humming a tune. It was only later that he recognized it as "Someone To Watch Over Me."

Mary Elizabeth Reardon died in her sleep the following day.

CHAPTER 18

Edward was seated on the couch with Steve watching The Lion King for perhaps the thirtieth time in the last six months. It was Steve's favorite movie; they watched it together at least once a week. He never seemed to tire of it, nor of telling his father what was going to happen next.

"This is the part where the daddy lion gets killed," he said.

"Mufasa," said Edward.

"That's the daddy lion," said Steve.

"Right. The Lion King."

"He's trying to rescue Simba. That's his son."

"I see."

"I'm your son," said Steve pointing to his chest.

"You are indeed. Which makes me very happy…And why does the Lion King have to rescue his bright young son?"

"Because his son is playing somewheres where he shouldn't."

"Right. He was dis-o-bey-ing his parents…And he-e-e-re come the wildebeests."

"The King's brother makes them do it. Makes the hyenas scare the wildybeests because he wants to kill his brother and be king himself. His name is Scar; he's a really bad lion."

"Very bad," said Edward.

"I have a brother."

Edward turned and looked at his small son cradled beneath his arm.

"You remember him?"

"Yeah."

"You only saw him a few times. And you were very young. Maybe not even two yet."

"He's lots older."

"That's right."

"Green shirt," said Steve.

"His favorite shirt. It was a birthday present for his seventeenth birthday."

"He's not here anymore"

"No," said Edward. "He left. A long time ago."

"I see him sometimes."

"You do?" said Edward.

"This is the part," said Steve, pointing to the television, "where the baby lion gets away and the hyenas can't follow him because he goes through the thorn bushes."

"You mean you remember seeing him? Tommy."

"At night sometimes."

"...You see him at night?"

"He wears that green shirt...Look, Daddy, there's Timon and Pumbaa."

In the movie, the wart hog and the meerkat were just discovering the exhausted Simba.

"You dream about him?" said Edward. "About Tommy."

"No."

Edward was quiet while Steve sang "Hakuna Matata." He knew all the words.

"I see him at night after I go to bed," said Steve.

154

"Ah, you see him at night," said Edward, nodding as if he understood, then looking up toward the ceiling for a possible answer.

You're doing just fine, said Sarah.
…But…
Just fine.

"But not dreaming? Not sleeping and dreaming?"

"No…You know in the movie when the daddy lion is up in the sky and tells Simba that it's time to go home?"

"Yeah."

"Like that."

"He just…appears? In the sky?"

"In my bedroom," said Steve, without taking his eyes off the television.

"Does he say anything?" said Edward.

"No. He puts his finger to his lips, like *shush*, when you want people to be quiet." Steve put his index finger to his lips and said *shhhhh*.

Edward slouched down on the couch so he was almost at eye level with his son.

"Wow…"

They watched the movie in silence for a few minutes.

"Why do you think he does that?" said Edward.

Steve shrugged.

"Maybe he doesn't want anybody to know he's there." he said.

"You sure it's him?" said Edward.

"Yeah."

"How can you tell?"

Steve shrugged again.

"I can tell," he said.

"Man," said Edward, shaking his head.

Out of the mouths of babes, said Sarah.

. . .How can that happen?

Oh, you Level Ones. You're all so mystified by the simplest things. That must be why I'm so fond of you.

"Do you ever try to talk to him?" said Edward.

"No."

"And he never says anything to you."

"No," said Steve. "He just smiles mostly."

"Does he seem happy?"

"...I guess."

. . .Hakuna matata, said Sarah.

"Jesus," said Edward, rubbing his forehead with his left hand.

"This is where the monkey teacher comes and tells Simba to go back home because the people need him really bad."

"Bad-ly."

"Bad-ly. They're starving and there's no lights."

"It's dark," said Edward.

"The hyenas turned out all the lights because of Scar."

"I was afraid of the dark when I was litttle."

"Me, too," said Steve. "When I was little."

"Dinner in five minutes, boys," Pam called from the kitchen. "Raviolio's."

"Oh, boy," said Steve. "Raviolio's."

"Oh, boy, Raviolio's. Again. My favorite."

In the movie, Simba was beginning the long journey back to the Pride Lands to face his nemesis, Scar and take his place as the rightful ruler.

"Are we Irish?" said Stevie.

"Of course. All the Gallaghers are Irish."

"What's sandy Irish?"

"Sandy Irish...Where did you hear that?"

"The teacher said it in class. We were learning about people who came to America from other places."

"Maybe shanty Irish?" said Edward.

"...Yeah. Shandy."

"They're poor folks who live in shanties, little shacks. Little houses,"

"Are we poor, daddy?"

"No."

"Are we rich?"

"No, we're right in the middle—just right. We have everything we need. There's you and me and mommy; that's all we'll ever need."

"...And Tommy," said Steve.

"Sure," he said, coughing as his eyes began to fill with tears. "Tommy. Of course."

"Dinner, boys," said Pam.

"You go ahead," said Edward, getting up and heading for the bathroom. "I'm gonna clean up."

Steve scampered off toward the kitchen and Edward headed for the bathroom to splash water on his face.

. . .Sarah? . . .Sarah? . .

There was no answer, though he did detect a small white light over his left shoulder when he looked in the bathroom mirror.

CHAPTER 19

Mr. Hall's new roommate looked to be a comparatively young man, no older than perhaps forty or forty-five. Brain cancer had rendered him blind, though his vocal chords were unaffected.

"What's your name?" said Mr. Hall, trying to be friendly.

"I'm blind, you know. Can't see a thing."

"That so?"

"Yeah. Been blind for I don't know how long. Got up one day and couldn't see. Just like that."

"...What'd you say your name was?" said Mr. Hall.

"Pine," said his roommate.

"Pine?"

"P-i-n-e. Like the tree. You don't hear good?"

"I hear fine," said Mr. Hall defensively. "Pine, eh?"

"That's it," said Mr. Pine. "You know me? Know who I am?"

"Just the name—Pine."

"Pine as in fine," said Mr. Pine. "Your name, sir?"

"Hall...What's your first name?"

"Charley. I'm Charley Pine, King of the Hill."

Mr. Hall looked over at his new roommate.

"Huh...King of the Hill, eh?"

Mr. Pine smiled and shook his head.

"Unfortunately, there's hardly any call for blind kings anymore. You blind?"

"I can still see some."

"What do I look like?" said Mr. Pine.

Mr. Hall pushed the button that raised the upper part of his bed, fumbled with his glasses and took a look.

"Can't tell how tall you are layin' down."

"Five foot ten, give or take a little...You?"

"Was six foot one," said Mr. Hall, "but I shrunk some."

"Are you old?"

"Old enough. And not fixin' to get much older they tell me."

"Me neither. Go on."

"Go on with what?"

"With what I look like."

"You want the truth?" said Mr. Hall.

"You mean I don't look like I should be in the movies?"

"Not hardly. Leastways it don't look like you're the Clark Gable type."

"Darn. Give me the rest of the bad news."

"Well...You got kind of a narrow face. Pointy chin. Nose is crooked. Bent some...I never described nobody's face before."

"You're doing fine. But you wouldn't go so far as to call me handsome?"

"Handsome," said Mr. Hall. "Hell, I don't have no idea what handsome looks like. Ask one of the nurses. Alberta or Vivian. Maybe Mary."

Mr. Pine touched his face with both hands.

"You know I can't remember what I look like. I looked in the mirror all those years, shaved every day, combed my hair, and now I can't remember what I look like. I don't even know if I'm real anymore. That's why I try to get people to tell me what I look like—so I can remember."

"Well, I don't suppose you're all that bad lookin'," said Mr. Hall. "You been blind long?"

"I don't think so, but it's hard to tell. Time's not what it used to be. I used to be able to count the mornings, the days, the nights. I did things. Went places. Things happened. I had a calendar right on the wall where I could take a look at it, track my way through the week. Okay, Tuesday is the day the dog goes to the vet. Thursday morning I have coffee with Gordon. Friday is a meeting. I have calendars from years ago— sometimes I'd go back and see what I did in December of '85. Now…Time's not the same."

"Like when I retired," said Mr. Hall. "Things was just different. Time moved different."

"Retire," said Mr. Pine. "I won't live long enough to retire. They told me, Get-your-affairs-in-order. That's when I knew it was over. You been retired long?"

"Long enough. I'm eighty-some now."

"I'm half your age—forty-one. What I wouldn't give to have another forty years. What'd you do before you retired?"

"I played some ball. Then carpenter work mostly. You?"

"I was a teacher," said Mr. Pine.

"That so," said Mr. Hall. "What'd you teach?"

"History. Russian history."

"We goin' to war with them? With the Russkies?"

"Not likely. They've fallen on hard times."

Mr. Hall stared at his roommate for a few moments, then held up his left hand with two fingers extended like a victory sign.

"How many fingers you see?" he said.

Mr. Pine turned his face toward the voice.

"…Eight?" he said.

"Nope."

"You think I can see?" said Mr. Pine. "That it? You're tryin' to find out if I can really see?"

"You got your eyes open."

Mr. Pine touched his eyes with his fingertips.

"So I do," he said. "You'd be surprised, but it's hard to tell if your eyes are open or closed when you can't see. You'd think it would be easy, but it's not. But I bet there's lots of people with their eyes open who can't see much of anything. You suppose?"

"Maybe," Mr. Hall said cautiously. "I worked hard all those years before I retired. Never sick a day."

"Until now."

"Until now…But you know the years go fast. Been better if somebody'd a told me that, about how fast they'd go." He tried to snap his fingers, but he was too weak. "Before you know it they're gone and you're eighty instead of forty. Old. Time runs out. You wonder where it went. The time. The years." He shrugged at the mystery of it all. "Just gone."

"Still," said Mr. Pine. "…I wouldn't mind having the extra forty, fast or not."

Mr. Hall sighed but didn't say anything.

"What if you got a chance to do it all over again," said Mr. Pine. "Your life. You ever think about that? Would you change anything?"

"…Some things," he said after a long pause.

"Like what?"

"Oh…I had a wife once wasn't worth much. The middle one—Effie. Run off one night and never come back. Just run off. Not so much as a phone call. I'd make sure I didn't marry her again. Then there was the car wreck. Nineteen and thirty six I believe. Comin' down the Grapevine near Bakersfield. You know where it is?"

"Yeah."

"Two of my best friends got killed. Throwed right outta the car."

"...That's strange," said Mr. Pine. "They tell me that's how my grandfather died—in a car wreck on the Grapevine. My grandfather and his brother. Sometime in the thirties. My father was just a baby when it happened. Says he doesn't remember ever seeing his father. Just pictures. Pictures and the stories my grandmother told him."

"Huh..." said Mr. Hall. "What was your grandaddy's name?"

"I don't remember," said Mr. Pine. "My father just called him Dad. All we had were the pictures and some stories."

"What'd he look like?"

"I can't tell what people look like anymore. Not since I've been blind. It's like I've lost part of my memory, too. I can still remember events, but I can't describe them, can't tell you what things actually looked like. When you ask about my grandfather, I can't tell what he looked like, even though I've seen the pictures."

"What about the stories?"

"Plenty of those," said Mr. Pine. "Evidently he was quite a hell raiser. My grandmother used to say, "That Jake...Jake, that's it. That was his name."

"Jake Pine," said Mr. Hall, slowly shaking his head. "Don't that beat all. John Marshall Pine."

"You knew him? Knew my grandfather?"

"I...knew him. Yeah."

"You were friends?"

"Acquaintances I guess you'd say."

"I remember it now," said Mr. Pine. "He had a brother named Arnie. Both killed in that car wreck. Arnie and Jake and ...somebody else. Somebody else who survived. I never heard who—just that he was a baseball player. Somebody famous was the way I got it from grandma."

"She say it like that?" said Mr. Hall. "Somebody famous?"

"I don't know if she actually said famous, but that's the impression I got."

162

"What'd she tell you about the wreck? How it happened and all?"

"Not much. Happened just over the crest of a hill. Somebody coming up the hill swerved into their lane on a wet street and hit them head on. They were driving an old Model A. The other car was a big Packard or something. Jake and Arnie were killed and the driver...somehow the driver survived with hardly a scratch on him."

"But the way you heard it the other car was over in their lane? The Packard?"

"That's what they said. I guess what the accident report said. Or the newspaper. But it's hard to say. If half the things they said about grandad were true, he might have been driving from the back seat."

"What's your grandma's name?"

"Martha."

"She still alive?"

"No. She passed on last year."

Mr. Hall looked out the window at the birds clustered around the bird feeder.

"Martha Pine," he said softly. "You're so fine."

"I'm sorry," said Mr. Pine. "I didn't hear you. I think my hearing's starting to go, too."

"Oh...Just mumblin' to myself. Bad habit I got lately. Your daddy still around?"

"No. Died a couple of years ago. Lung cancer."

"Sorry to hear that," said Mr. Hall.

Just then Edward pushed the Cocktail Cart into the room, loose bottles clinking noisily.

. . .Wait till you hear this story, said Sarah.

Which story is that?

This one right here. Remember Mr. Hall talking about the two people who were killed in the car wreck? Jake and Arnie Pine? His two buddies?

163

Yeah. . .

Well, said Sarah, a note of triumph in her voice. This is Jake's grandson.

This Mr. Pine here? He's Jake's grandson?. .You have anything to do with this, Sarah?

. . . Maybe a little.

What happened to only being able to change minor things like temperature and wind velocity?

Well. . .there are always exceptions, Edward. Emergency situations, so to speak. I had to get a special dispensation for this one. Desperate measures and so forth. . .

"What's that noise?" said Mr. Pine, looking in Edward's direction.

"Oh, that's just the whiskey cart," said Mr. Hall.

"It's me," said Edward, "with your room service cart. Cocktails, soda pop, wine, whiskey, chocolate, munchies, whatever appeals to you."

"This here's Charley Pine," said Mr. Hall, introducing his roommate.

"And I'm Ed Gallagher, your personal bartender."

"Mr. Pine here's blind," said Mr. Hall.

"Can't see a thing," said Mr. Pine. "It's nighttime all the time. Are you blind, Ed Gallagher? Old maybe?"

"Well," said Edward, "I'm not blind, though I need glasses to read. And I'm fifty years old. I don't know if that's old or not. Mr. Hall would probably think that's young."

"It's older than I am," said Mr. Pine. "Older than I'm ever going to be."

"Could I get you a glass of wine before dinner?" said Edward.

"Is dinner soon?"

"Forty-five minutes maybe."

"What are we having?"

"I hardly ever check the menu," said Edward. "But most

likely it's some soup and a little stew. Plain but nourishing is what they say in the kitchen. Then custard or jello for dessert."

"I'm not very hungry."

"That's okay," said Mr. Hall. "Dinner probably don't taste like much anyway so it'll work out just fine."

"Glass of wine might help your appetite," said Edward.

"You know, one of the worst things about being blind is that it's hard to know what you're eating. Even after they tell me what it is and I taste it, I still can't tell."

"I can help you with that," said Mr. Hall. "I could explain it, your dinner. Tell you what it is and all. Describe it."

"They'll have somebody come in and help feed you," said Edward. "Make it a little easier."

"But I could do that," said Mr. Hall. "Like I said. You could get me into a wheelchair and push me over by the bed. I can work a fork and spoon good as anybody. And they don't feed nothin' here requires a knife. Just mush and custard and stew."

"Mr. Hall here knew my grandfather," said Mr. Pine. "They were...acquaintances you said?"

"We was in school together."

Mr. Hall looked at Edward and put his forefinger to his lips.

"That makes it almost a family thing, doesn't it?" said Mr. Pine. "I don't have any family left. No kids, no kinfolk. One ex-wife who lives in New Jersey and never wants to see me again. Can't count her. So I show up here and find a friend of grandad's. What are the chances of that happening?"

"Pretty slim," said Edward. "As a matter of fact it's almost ...miraculous."

...Amen, said Sarah. And thanks for the plug. . .
You're welcome. . .

"We have a nice Chablis or a Zinfandel," said Edward.

165

"Might perk up your appetite."

"The other thing I hate about being blind is that you have to sit down to take a pee. You probably never thought about that, being able to see and all. You could stand up. I never thought about it either. Not till lately. Just doesn't seem right."

"You think that's bad," said Mr. Hall, "you oughta try one of these catherator things. Sittin' to take a pee's most likely a breeze compared to this."

Edward poured half a glass of Chablis and set it on the tray next to Mr. Pine's bed.

"Here's a little glass of wine," said Edward. "It's on the tray next to the right side of your bed. When you're ready, I'll put it in your hand. It's only about half full."

"I'll wait," said Mr. Pine. "Maybe have it later."

"And when dinner comes," said Mr. Hall, "you'll come back and get me into my wheelchair so I can help Mr. Charley Pine here?"

"I will," said Edward. "Something off the Cocktail Cart for you, Mr. Hall?"

"Maybe a soda pop," said Mr. Hall. "I got feedin' duty tonight." He winked at Edward. "One glass of wine and I might stick a spoonful of somethin' in his ear. Might not sit too well with Mr. Charley Pine."

Edward opened a Mountain Dew, put it on the tray next to Mr. Hall's bed and went about his appointed rounds.

When dinner was served, he got Mr. Hall into his wheelchair, pushed him over to Mr. Pine's bed and got him started with the feeding.

"Should I come back in a bit and take you out for a smoke?" said Edward.

"Yeah," said Mr. Hall. "Half hour or so? We oughta be through by then."

Edward stood outside the door for a few moments and listened to the conversation.

166

"This here's some soup," said Mr. Hall.

"Is it hot?"

"Didn't feel hot."

"What kind?"

"White…with some lumps in it. White lumps. Might be potato soup."

"Did you taste it?" said Mr. Pine.

"No."

"How did you know if it was hot."

"I stuck my pinky in it."

"I hope your hands are clean."

"Well, I know my pinky is," said Mr. Hall.

"Did you know vodka was made from potatoes."

"That a fact? Open up, here comes the soup. They got lots of potatoes in Russia?"

"In the Ukraine."

"Open wide."

"Mmmm…Soup's not bad."

"They make a passable soup here," said Mr. Hall.

"Tell me what the room looks like."

"There's a dresser down by the foot of the bed. Big brown dresser. Two teevees. The two beds. Mirror over the dresser. Not all that much to it. Got a bird feeder outside the window. You can see them come…Well, they don't always come and there's not all that much to see anyway. Just little brown birds don't amount to much."

"But you could tell me when they come," said Mr. Pine. "Describe them. Tell me what they look like. Are there any birds there now?"

"No, it's gettin' on to dark now. They come mostly in the day."

"You'll have to tell me whether it's daytime or nighttime, too. I can't tell. That'll help, knowing when the sun's out."

"Open wide," said Mr. Hall. "Here comes some more tater soup."

167

Mr. Hall managed to get the spoonful in without spilling it.

"You know," said Mr. Pine, "I could probably take you out to the smoking room when we're through with dinner."

"Well, I don't know as how you could manage to..."

"You could direct me. I could push and you could tell me Right or Left or Straight Ahead. I could be the legs and you could be the eyes. My legs are still good. It's my eyes that don't work."

"Well...Might be okay," said Mr. Hall. "Don't suppose there's no rule sayin' we can't."

"I could be like a co-pilot," said Mr. Pine. "That way we could help each other. We could move around some. By ourselves."

"Open up again," said Mr. Hall. "Here comes the beef stew. Leastways I think it's beef."

Mr. Pine chewed thoughtfully for a few minutes while Mr. Hall stirred the soup.

"How's it taste?" he said.

"Not too bad," said Mr. Pine. "A little...cardboardy."

"That's a specialty here. Cardboardy stew with little pieces of spuds and carrots."

"Maybe I could get the recipe. Send it to my ex-wife."

"You know that thing with the wheelchair might just work," said Mr. Hall. "You pushin' and me navigatin'. That way we wouldn't have to wait for someone to take us out there. Wheel of Fortune's on just after dinner. You ever see it?"

"I have."

"We could watch together...I could explain the spaces, how many there was, and what letters been used, and you could help figure it out. Hell, you was a schoolteacher. You oughta be good at this."

"I was always good at crossword puzzles," said Mr. Pine.

"This'll be right up your alley. More stew?"

"Maybe a sip of wine first," said Mr. Pine. "Is it still there? On the tray?"

"Right here. Just hold out your hand."

Mr. Pine took the glass in both hands and brought it slowly to his lips.

"Your grandad was quite a guy," said Mr. Hall. "He just done a little too much social drinkin' for his own good is all. But we all did...I got another spoonful of that real good tater soup here. Just say the word."

"No, I think I've had about enough for tonight."

"Here, just one more spoonful. If you gonna be pushin' this wheelchair around, we gotta be sure to keep up your strength. I don't wanna get started and run outta gas somewhere in the middle of nowheres."

"Well. . .Maybe one more."

"You know I been thinkin'," said Mr Hall. "About what you look like and all. I think you could play Clark Gable in one of them long distance scenes. Like way over by the fence. Or ridin' a horse off in the distance."

"They get the camera far enough away, *you* could play Clark Gable."

"Not likely," said Mr. Hall, chuckling. "I look like the guy who played Pa in the Ma and Pa Kettle movies. All wrinkled up."

Edward smiled and continued on his rounds, pushing the cart down the hallway toward the next room, bottles clinking merrily against one another.

CHAPTER 20

When Bingo was on the Activities Calendar, Mrs. McKelvey could hardly wait to get to the Family Room; she went rolling up and down the hallway in her wheelchair announcing the event as if it had national significance.

Mr. Pine and Mr. Hall were still getting used to their new tandem arrangement, one pushing, one navigating. . .*Little more to the right, more, more, that's good. Straight ahead, Watch the door!. . .I can't see. . .Oh, yeah. Just go easy now. . .* Edward helped Mr. Barnett down the hallway and into one of the easy chairs—he was very weak. Mary Blanchard sat with him, holding his hand and occasionally whispering something in his ear that made him smile. Mrs. Muggeridge arrived in a swirl of chiffon, still painfully thin, though looking more vital than ever; she actually seemed to be getting better. Tony carried Miss Gladys in and set her at one end of the couch, knowing she would want to come and Praise Jesus in a crowd. She smiled broadly, all purple gums and no teeth, knowing that she and the Baby Jesus would soon be together. Mr. Ambrose came thumping along, hair wild as ever, a green, inflatable donut draped around his neck like a floral wreath. Eldon made it under his own power, though he seemed to be going downhill quickly, barely able to shuffle along. Everytime Miss Glady said Praise Jesus, Eldon countered with something about the Great Pumpkin.

"Welcome to Bingo," said Mrs. Toller, her voice a rising crescendo of enthusiasm. "I'm assuming everyone knows how to play."

"This like reg'lar Bingo?" said Mr. Ambrose.

"Exactly," said Mrs. Toller.

"Like E-four and D-six? Like that?"

"Exactly."

"It's just like regular Bingo," said Mrs. McKelvey. "Everybody knows how to play regular Bingo."

"Would you like to sit down, Mr. Ambrose?" said Mrs. Toller.

"I gotta stand up," he said. "My piles are killin' me. Donut or not, they're killin' me."

"Is there a prize if we win?" said Mrs. Muggeridge.

"Of course," said Mrs. Toller. "We have a very nice fruit basket from Safeway, and as an added bonus, a small bag of goodies."

"Thank God," said Mrs. Muggeridge. "Something beside this awful food. I can't imagine how they sleep nights, feeding us like this. Don't any of them have a conscience? Someone should call the police."

"Hey po-lice," croaked Mr. Barnett, smiling broadly.

"Potato soup wasn't so bad the other night," said Mr. Pine. "Or the stew even."

"A little cardboardy was all," added Mr. Hall. "But not that bad."

"I must have been out dancing that night," said Mrs. Muggeridge.

"You know I can't see anymore," said Mr. Pine.

"How do you know what you're eating?" said Mrs.

Muggeridge.

"My pal here tells me," he said, pointing in the general direction of Mr. Hall.

Mr. Hall smiled and nodded.

"And I describe it," he said.

"You all have your Bingo cards?" said Mrs. Toller.

"Do I?" said Mr. Pine.

"You do," said Mr. Hall. "Right on the table next to mine. I'll do 'em together."

"I never played Bingo," said Mr. Pine.

"Easy as pie," said Mr. Hall.

"Everybody knows how to play Bingo," said Mrs. McKelvey.

"You suppose they have Braille Bingo?"

"They do," said Mrs. Toller, making a notation on her pad. "We don't have one at the moment, but the cards are on order."

"I can't read Braille anyway," said Mr. Pine. "I've only been blind for awhile. Not all that long. Not long enough to learn Braille."

"Lotta gui-tar players was blind," offered Mr. Barnett in his flat mechanical monotone. "Blind Le-mon Je-ffer-son, Blind Boy Fu-ller…"

"Ronnie Milsap," said Mary Blanchard.

"…Who?"

"Ronnie Milsap," she said. "Country."

"Country's not mu-sic," he said.

"You ever hear of Charley Pride?" she said.

"Oh, man," he said with a soundless chuckle.

"I don't play guitar either," said Mr. Pine. "I was a teacher. A history teacher."

"I don't see too good," said Mr. Ambrose, "but I don't think I'm blind."

"You'd know if you were," said Mr. Pine. "Believe me. It's dark. Completely dark."

"Blind," said Mrs. Muggeridge. "It must be awful. For all

you know, they could be feeding you toads for dinner."

"Really," said Mrs. Toller. "I don't think it's all that appetizing to be talking about toads before dinner."

"Not only that," said Mr. Pine, "but I have to sit down to take a pee. I find that very distressing."

"Oh, you'll get used to it," Mrs. McKelvey said cheerfully. "I've been doing it for years."

"And I'm here to be sure he won't be eatin' no toads," said Mr. Hall. "This boy here is the grandson of one of my old classmates. I'm takin' care of him."

"How nice," said Mrs. Toller. "What a small world."

"Praise Jesus," said Miss Gladys.

"And the Great Pumpkin, amen," said Eldon.

You think I'll have time to learn all my lessons this time around?

What brings this on?

When I see these people here, I wonder if. . .

There's always plenty of what you call Time, Edward, because Time doesn't really exist. It's a, for lack of a better term, a Level One concept. A handy device, but not to be taken seriously. You know the minutes, hours, days thing? Doesn't exist. That's why it sometimes seems to go fast, and sometimes seems to go slow.

I don't understand. . .

You see, Edward, all this is wonderful camouflage. The world as you know it? What you see around you? Camouflage. It's all happening inside and being projected out there. . .like a movie. It works from the inside out. All very simple.

Why do I get this sense of panic every time you say simple?

Because you're thinking too much. Trying to figure it out. Didn't we discuss that?

. . .But how can I possibly be creating all this. . .

How do I get into these long theoretical discussions you seem to love so much? The Why and the How of it. It will all have to wait, Edward. If you'll pardon the pun—No time for it now.

"Everybody ready?" said Mrs. Toller, reaching into the shallow Melmac bowl with the numbered balls in it. "Here goes. ...E-Three. .."

"Bingo," said Mr. Ambrose, cackling noisily. "Bongo bongo, I don't wanna leave the Congo..."

"Surely you can't have Bingo already," said Mrs. McKelvey. "We've only had one number."

"Ha ha," said Mr. Ambrose. "April Fools. I seen that in a movie one time."

"I got E-Three?" said Mr. Pine.

"Nope," said Mr. Hall. "Me, neither."

"You sure?"

"Sure I'm sure. Don't take no Einstein to figure out E-Three. It's there or it ain't."

"Me and the Great Pumpkin have it," said Eldon. His face was flushed and his breathing labored, though he still managed a smile. His chest cold was rapidly turning into pneumonia.

"Who's the Great Pumpkin?" said Mr. Pine.

"I wouldn't have no possible idea," said Mr. Hall.

"The Great Pumpkin is a little like what most people think of as God," said Eldon. "Only better. He brings toys to all the little boys and girls. He's like God and Santa Claus all wrapped up in one."

"Praise Jesus," said Miss Gladys. "Nothin' better'n God."

"Next number," Mrs. Toller said quickly, hoping to avoid a confrontation between God and the Great Pumpkin. "...G-Six."

"Oh, my," said Mrs. Muggeridge. "That's me. Three more good numbers and I can get a basket of fruit. And some... goodies, did you say?"

"Right," said Mrs. Toller. "Some goodies."

"What kind of goodies?" said Mrs. Muggeridge.

"Oh, we must have some surprises, don't you think?

174

Wouldn't it be dull if we didn't have any surprises?"

"I'm really surprised," said Mr. Ambrose.

"At what?" said Mrs. Toller.

"At how dull it is when there's no surprises…Ha ha ha."

"Everybody got G-Six?" said Mrs. Toller.

"The Great Pumpkin's got it," said Eldon.

"And Mr. Charley Pine here's got it, too," said Mr. Hall.

"How many more numbers I need?" said Mr. Pine.

"Gotta have three more in that same row," said Mr. Hall.

"Or diagonally," said Mrs. McKelvey.

"Right," said Mr. Hall. "Or catty-wampus. Either way."

Mrs. Toller rattled the numbered balls in the Melmac bowl and picked another one.

"Next number…A-Three…"

"…A-Three?" said Mrs. Muggeridge.

Mrs Toller looked at the ball again.

"Right. A-Three."

"Shit," said Mr. Ambrose. "Pardon my French. I ain't got a one yet."

"The Great Pumpkin strikes again," said Eldon. "I only need one more. O Great Pumpkin, thank you for. . ."

"Praise Jesus, Praise Jesus, Praise Jesus," said Miss Gladys, shaking her head as if to drown out his voice.

"I'd settle for just one number," said Mr. Ambrose. "Any number. Just one simple number."

"Trouble is," said Eldon, "the minute you got one number, you'd want another one. And then another one. It's human nature."

Mr. Ambrose scratched the back of his neck and thought about that for a moment.

"Prob'ly so," he said. "Havin' two numbers'd be okay. Three even. I don't see nothin' wrong with wantin' another number."

"How're we doing?" said Mr. Pine.

"Two out of three," said Mr. Hall. "I got the same, but they

175

don't line up with nothin'. I need some in-between numbers."

"I could concentrate better if I had a bourbon and orange juice," said Mrs. McKelvey.

"Right after the game," said Mrs.Toller. "Everybody ready for the next number?"

"You remember King Kong?" said Mr. Ambrose.

"...The movie?" said Mrs. McKelvey.

"Yeah. That was the first time I took Piggy out," he said. "Our first date. To see that movie. I'd already seen it three, maybe four times. I was eighteen and she was...seventeen maybe." He gazed out the window where the small brown finches were gathering at the bird feeder. "Nineteen and thirty-eight, and I was workin' for Goodyear. Before the War."

"Piggy was...your wife?" said Mrs. Toller.

"Later she was," said Mr. Ambrose.

"That was her real name? Piggy?"

"No, Peggy was her real name. I just called her Piggy for short. Scared the bejesus outa her."

"What did?"

"The movie. You ever see it?"

"I don't think so."

"It's about this fifty foot gorilla that lives on Skull Island."

"Skull Island?" said Mrs. Toller.

"Where King Kong lives," he said. "In the movie. It was way out in the ocean somewheres. I remember all those things. Details like that stick in my mind like glue. I got the memory of a person twice my age. Gigantic. Twice my age easy."

"Oh, praise sweet Jesus," said Miss Gladys.

Mr. Ambrose put both hands on the inflatable donut draped around his neck, teetered unsteadily for a moment before he had to put one hand back on his walker to steady himself.

"King Kong was a killer," he said dramatically. "The terror of the civilized world. Human sacrifice was his game."

"Ugh," said Mrs. Muggeridge.

"The Great Pumpkin is more powerful than King Kong,"

said Eldon. He seemed feverish. Mary Blanchard watched him closely.

"Nobody's more powerful than King Kong," said Mr. Ambrose.

"Can he fly?" said Eldon.

"...I don't think so."

"The Great Pumpkin can fly."

"Remember when he got hold of that lady?" said Mr. Ambrose. "The one who plays the actress?"

"Fay something," said Eldon.

"That's right," he said. "Fay Somethin'. Had her in the palm of his hand. In the palm of his hand. That's how big he was."

"I used to think about that," said Eldon.

"...About what?"

"About how big he was."

"I saw King Kong," said Mr. Pine. "Long time ago. When I could still see. On teevee. I cheered when the gorilla got hold of the girl. My wife thought I was very insensitive. My ex-wife. She had absolutely no sense of humor. I never had good luck with women."

"Me neither," said Eldon.

"Men," said Mrs. Muggeridge, shaking her head. "My husband was a toll collector in the Holland Tunnel for thirty-three years...And then he died, God rest his soul. Thirty-three years and then he died. It was all those fumes, but of course they'll never pay off...Bastards."

"He-e-e-e-re comes the next number," said Mrs. Toller. "Everybody check your cards now...B-Six."

"A near miss," said Eldon.

"Hey, I got one," said Mr. Ambrose. "Hope I'm not too late."

"Too late for what?" said Eldon.

"Too late to win."

"You're never too late to win," said Mrs. Toller. "Long as

177

you keep trying, you've got a chance. That's what my third grade teacher, Mrs. Martin, always said. I never forgot."

"What happened to the lady," said Mrs. Muggeridge. "Did the gorilla kill her?"

"No," said Mr. Ambrose. "He let her go. Big as he was, he was a softy at heart. A fifty foot marshmellow. But he did try to take her clothes off."

"God help us," said Mrs. Muggeridge.

"Praise Jesus," said Miss Gladys.

Several more numbers were called before the winner came up.

"The next number," said Mrs. Toller. "...B-Three."

"Hey, I got another number," said Mr. Ambrose. "Two more in the same row and I got a winner."

"*Bingo!*" said Eldon, thrusting a fist in the air.

"That mean I'm too late?" said Mr. Ambrose.

A collective groan greeted the news.

"I only needed one more," said Mr. Hall.

"Thank you, Great Pumpkin," said Eldon.

"And me?" said Mr. Pine. "Wasn't I close?"

"One more for you, too."

"Oh, my," said Mrs. Muggeridge.

Mr. Barnett just chuckled through his voice box—he sometimes sounded like a toy fog horn.

"Did I tell you how it ends?" said Mr. Ambrose.

"...How what ends?" said Mrs. Toller.

"The movie."

"No."

"He gets killed. The gorilla. He's climbin' on the Umpire State Buildin' and he falls off. They got airplanes flyin' all over makin' him very nervous. He's tryin' to knock 'em down when he falls. But later they had a movie called The Return of King Kong, so it turns out he wasn't dead after all. Just hurt bad."

"Monsters never die," said Eldon. "Look at all the Frankenstein movies. And Dracula."

178

"Dracula's a vampire," said Mr. Ambrose. "Can't kill vampires. Besides, strictly speakin', King Kong wasn't a monster."

"Is it four o'clock yet," said Mrs. McKelvey.

"Almost," said Mrs. Toller.

"Wonder what it would be like to be a vampire," said Mr. Ambrose. "Live forever."

"You have to drink blood to stay alive," said Eldon. "Kill people and drink their blood."

"Ugh…" said Mrs. Muggeridge.

"Vampire's prob'ly don't get piles," said Mr. Ambrose. "Be worth a couple of glasses of blood to get rid of the piles."

"Wonderful game," said Mrs. Toller. "Very competitive. Here's the fresh fruit basket and the bag of goodies for Eldon."

Mary started the applause and the others joined in.

Eldon shuffled painfully to the front of the room, took the basket of fruit, turned and gave it to Mrs. Muggeridge.

"For you, ma'm," said Eldon with a courtly bow. "A basket of fruit…Something to remember me by."

"Why, thank you," said Mrs. Muggeridge. "That's very generous."

"It's over?" said Mr. Pine. "The game? Can we play again? I almost won, didn't I?"

"Very close," said Mr. Hall. "Very, very close."

"We'll play again soon," said Mrs. Toller. "Don't worry. Mrs. McKelvey will round you all up for another game soon."

"I know a song," said Mr. Ambrose. "We could all sing." He started off in a raspy baritone. . .

"Row, row, row your boat. . ."

Mrs. Toller waved her arms like a choir director urging the others to join in.

". . .Gently down the stre-e-e-e-am. . .

Merrily, merrily, merrily, merrily, life is but a dream. . ."

. . .Is it? said Edward.

179

Is it what? said Sarah.

Is it a dream? Life?

That's a very complicated question, Edward. Difficult to explain with Level One language limitations. We might discuss it before the book is finished. But then. . .

What book? said Edward

The one you're going to write about all this.

. . .God. . .I'm going home and rest.

Good idea, said Sarah.

I'll see you next week.

You will indeed. But if you need me, I'm never far away. You just have to ask.

. . .I don't understand any of this.

I know. And it's better that way. It's not necessary that you understand right now. Just keep moving, Edward. See how the scenery changes when you're moving?

CHAPTER 21

When Edward went to the hospice the following week, he discovered that Eldon had been put on Watch. He had often wondered if Eldon used the Great Pumpkin the way Edward used the Force; as a handy substitute for a Word that had come to mean Judgment, Damnation and Guilt—a Word that carried with it the weight of all his childhood fears and insecurities. God would indeed get-him (he had always know that); it was just a matter of time, given his own curiosity, his penchant for experimentation, and his natural stubborness that made all rules look like fences begging to be jumped.

How many nights had he lain abed with his mind firmly around some sexual fantasy, praying for guidance while stacking the deck in favor of pleasure even before the first false prayer had risen from his lips? Too many, he decided, sealing his fate long before the first sweet rose docked in his garden.

He began the rounds that afternoon with a heavy heart.

. . .*Why so glum? said Sarah.*

Oh. . .I don't know. Maybe it's Eldon. I think about him and the Great Pumpkin a lot.

You mean the God thing?

Maybe. . .I don't know.

If it's any comfort, he's going home now. He'll rest up and be back.

That's part of what's so depressing, said Edward. I mean you do one life, then you do another. Maybe it's Auschwitz one time and AIDS the next. What kind of deal is that?

I won't try to explain it, because there are no words to go with it. Level Ones are purposely not equipped to understand. That's so you'll take it seriously enough to learn the lessons. Otherwise, you'd be giggling all the time. So today, as a special treat, you're going to experience a little of what God is. Or the Force. Or the Great Pumpkin. Names are just names. This is a little show and tell. Only a little, because if you get too much you'll just burst into flames. I've seen that happen. You have to be careful.

. . .I'm going to experience what God is? said Edward.

Only a little, said Sarah. In this case too much of a good thing isn't good for you.

But how. . .

Hush, said Sarah. No more questions. Go about your rounds and see what happens.

Edward filled the ice bucket from the ice machine in the kitchen and rolled the cart slowly down the hallway. There were new names on the doors he passed—Ethyl Coleman, Anita Bonnano, Pietro Franconi, Nathan Ridley. The patients arrived, stayed awhile and died. Some were there for weeks or months, some for only a day or two. The dead were brought to the Blue Room, properly mourned by those who loved them, then spirited away in ambulances, the bodies now cold and stiff. Some were sent to mortuaries where they would be pumped full of fluids to make them look as if they were only

182

sleeping, some went to be cremated, reduced to ashes and placed in small, ornate containers.

Sometimes it just got to him. In the last month or so many of his favorites had gone—Mrs.Watkins, Mrs. Reardon, Mr. and Mrs. Borstein, Mrs. Mathews, David Sparrowhawk. Those recently arrived would follow the same route.

. . .Cheer up, said Sarah. The last thing these people need is a depressing bartender.

I was just thinking. . .

Again. We've been all over that, Edward. You think too much. Especially about yourself. What did we decide the antidote was. . .?

God, you're such a pain, Sarah. You know that? You're so . . .relentless.

Thank you. And the antidote is?. . .thinking about someone else for a change. Doing something for someone else. Being of service.

I know, I know, said Edward.

Knowing's not enough. People who know are cheap on the open market. There are lots of very smart people out there who know things. But it's action we're after, Edward. Service is love in action. Love without action is sympathy. At best. So be about your business. I'll be nearby.

"How is it today, Mrs. Muggeridge?" he said.

She was standing in front of the window watching the birds at the feeder.

"I wonder what they feed the birds?" she asked. "Must be very good because they're flying all around. You'd think they could feed us as well, wouldn't you. Do you know what's for dinner tonight, young man?"

"I'm not sure but I think it's grilled cheese sandwiches and some kind of custard."

Her shoulders sagged visibly.

183

"Oh, my…The cheese is like glue I bet. It always is. I can't swallow it."

"I can get some extra custard, Mrs. Muggeridge. Or get the kitchen to make you something different."

She waved the suggestion away with a hand that looked more like a claw.

"No matter," she said. "I can't eat anyway."

She turned from the window and looked at him—hers was a delicate beauty, heightened by her pale complexion, the translucent quality of her skin.

"I'm…fading you know. Each day a little more. I can feel it. Each day I have less and less energy. Fading like the last rose of summer. Soon…" she turned her palms up in a gesture of helplessness, "there won't be anything left. Now I lay me down to die. You ever hear that? It's an old poem I think. I don't remember the rest."

She walked around the bed toward Edward.

"Do you know what it feels like to be dying?"

"…No."

"It feels like a little more of your spirit leaves every day. Just goes off somewhere. You don't know where. There are days when I think I can actually hear the cancer spreading, like an army of small invaders consuming its host. Very unpleasant. It's a little harder to get out of bed, to make conversation, to walk across the room. My mind goes off somewhere for long periods. There are days when I want it to be over with as quickly as possible. I want to be in Heaven with the angels and the saints. With Frank. Dancing with Frank. Other days I'm…afraid. On those days, I'm not sure about anything."

She looked straight at him with eyes that seemed to glow with intensity.

"Sometimes at night," she said, "when it's very dark and very quiet, I see a little light off in the distance."

. . .A-men, said Sarah.

184

Is that you?
You probably thought I slept at night. Somebody has to watch the Store, Edward.

"...What do you think it is?" said Edward.

"I think it's home," she said. "I think it's an angel lighting the way. And I think I'll be going home soon."

"You know it very well could be an angel...Would you like a drink, Mrs. Muggeridge. Before dinner. Some Peppermint Schnapps?"

"Do you have any Apricot Schnapps?"

Edward took a quick inventory of the supply on his cart. On the bottom shelf there was a nearly full bottle of Apricot Schnapps. Odd, he thought. He had never noticed it before.

"Here we are," he said, displaying the bottle.

"That's what Frank and I drank when we first met. Don't ask me why. I never met another soul who liked Apricot Schnapps. Or Peppermint Schnapps for that matter. You'd think we were German. Aren't they the ones who drink Schnapps? We were dancers, Frank and I. Ballroom dancers long before it was so popular. We did the waltz. Do you dance, young man?"

"I'm not much of a dancer," said Edward.

"It's not too late to learn," she said. "Here, I'll help you."

She assumed a dance position—right arm extended, left arm bent and elevated, waiting for her partner. He put the bottle down and took her in his arms; she seemed to weigh no more than the chiffon gown she wore.

"Now waltz is three-quarter time," she explained. "That means there are three beats to a measure. Tum ta ta, tum ta ta. ...Ready...start, Tum ta ta. . ."

They danced slowly in a small circular pattern. Though she didn't seem to be leading, he found that he was following her. She kept time...*Tum ta ta, Tum ta ta*...

"A little practice," she said, "and you could be a very good

185

dancer, young man."

"I have this feeling that you're making it look like I can dance. When in fact I really can't."

"Frank used to say we did it with mirrors."

But she had to stop after only a few minutes. She sat on the edge of the bed and put her hand to her heart.

"Oh my goodness me," she said.

"Thank you," said Edward.

"I believe I'll have that drink now, young man. Would you join me?"

"I might have a Pepsi," he said.

"Good. It may sound strange, but I have a very peaceful feeling now. Maybe it was the dancing. Old times…"

He poured the Apricot Schnapps over ice and opened a can of Pepsi for himself.

"Cheers," he said.

"*L'chaim*," she said.

He nodded.

"*L'chaim*."

She sipped a little of her drink, set the glass on the bedside tray and took a deep breath.

"It's coming from you," she said.

"…What's coming from me?"

"That sense of peace. It's coming from you."

"I…I can't imagine that's true," he said. "I've heard people say I create a fair amount of turmoil, but…"

"No," she said firmly. "It's coming from you."

My, my, my, said Sarah.
My my what?
Hush. . .and listen.

"My mother was Irish," said Mrs. Muggeridge, "and she used to call people like you fey. Do you know the word? I never heard anybody but my mother use it. Said people like that

186

were connected to the Little People who could cast spells, see the future."

"I don't think any of that really fits me," said Edward. "I'm not..."

Mrs. Muggeridge held up her hand.

"I know what I know," she said. "There's something about you that brings peace."

. . .Don't you love it that our Teachers show up in the strangest places? said Sarah. Teachers and Revealers—they're the ones who just say the words without knowing what they mean. The Source likes to pick Revealers that most people think aren't too bright—like children and old people. Just goes to show you that if you don't pay attention, you miss a lot. . .And you certainly don't have to be a Level Six to be a Teacher.

All I know right now, said Edward, is that I'm very confused.

Well, fasten your seat belt, because it's about to get even more confusing.

Mrs. Muggeridge yawned daintily and lay back on the bed.

"Remember what I said, young man. It's important. I'm going to take a nap now. I'll see you in the sweet bye and bye."

He touched her shoulder lightly. She smiled and closed her eyes. He pushed the Cart out of the room and started down the hallway.

. . .Better get to Eldon's room, said Sarah. He doesn't have much time left.

Edward left the Cocktail Cart outside the door when he got to Eldon's room. Eldon lay in bed with his eyes closed, his breathing ragged and shallow.

Hold his hand, said Sarah.

Edward pulled a chair close to the bed and took one of Eldon's hands in both of his.

. . .Now listen carefully, said Sarah. . .You have asked for guidance and it has been granted. For now, I want you to follow Eldon's breathing and create a white light inside yourself.
. . .Inside me where? said Edward.
Just inside, said Sarah. It will find its place.

Edward followed Eldon's breathing and thought about a white light. He closed his eyes and noticed that as his own breathing became slower, Eldon's followed until they were both breathing inside a white light which expanded and contracted with each breath. His awareness of time was gradually replaced by a deep sense of peace unlike anything he had ever experienced. The light itself seemed alive, endowed with richness and meaning. It was immense, powerful, yet personal and...somehow loving.

. . .What has been granted to you is a grace, said Sarah. A gift freely given. Your presence will bring peace. Mrs. Muggeridge was right. That grace, that peace, will pass through you and be a gift to others. It will heal old wounds, soothe and comfort those most in need.
. . .I'll be a. . .healer? said Edward.
Labels, said Sarah. Very dangerous. I have this feeling that if you really thought of yourself as a Healer, capital H, the next thing you'd want would be a large following and eventually a church. Robes and rituals. Incense and ceremonies. Money. It's the way those things happen. The power is very subtle but real. Try to think of yourself as a channel, it's not as dangerous that way.
That means I'll be here for awhile? said Edward. Doing

this. . .whatever it is I'm supposed to be doing?

The time of departure from the earth plane is not foreordained, said Sarah. Nobody leaves unless the time is agreed upon.

But why. . .

Remember that this is for others, Edward. You shall remain as anonymous as ever. Very few will know. That's as it should be. There was first a need for you to be empty and you have come to your emptiness honestly. Drugs and alcohol did for you what you would never allow a spiritual discipline to do—they beat you into a state of reasonableness. The Ground has been prepared. Defeat in that sense has many things to recommend it. Think of it as a Divine Hammer. You've paid your dues, endured the despair and hopelessness of many a dark night. As you're fond of saying, you've Done Your Time. And if nature abhors a vacuum, let it be known that God, or the Great Pumpkin, abhors one even more. If you are empty, this Power rushes in to fill the void. It's all very simple. . .Now be with Eldon while there is time. Because this, Edward, is what God is.

What do you mean, this is. . .

This is what God is, said Sarah. This. God's face is Eldon's face, Mary's face, Baby Rachelle's face, Mrs. Reardon's face. It's love and compassion. You don't have to go to church to find it. You just have to look around. The faces of God are everywhere.

I'm lost, said Edward.

Let yourself be lost, she said. Surrender. . .Your son Tommy is here now with us. He chose his life and knew the obstacles beforehand. As we all do. Though you and he have been together many times through the centuries; this was one of the most difficult lives for both of you. It would be a mistake to think that because he did not conquer his addictions that his life was a failure. There are no lives that are failures. He learned many valuable lessons. Your understanding of life is much too limited to judge failure or success. He picked an Arizona highway to make his exit, falling asleep at the wheel, dying instantly when he rolled his pickup. He made sure he was alone and that no one else would be hurt. He simply woke up on this side of the veil.

His Father's Day card to you was his attempt to heal that rift before he left. Even though you hadn't seen him for nearly a year, he wanted you to know that he loved you. His detour to Los Angeles on his way to Phoenix was a way to say goodbye to his mother. He knew without knowing that it was his time. He is a remarkable soul, filled with grace. He is a Teacher now who appears in dreams to help guide people through difficult times.

Without knowing why, Edward started to cry. He wept for perhaps five minutes, sobbing uncontrollably, then stopped suddenly when he felt Eldon squeeze his hand.

Tears cleanse and heal, said Sarah. . .They wash away old debris from cluttered lifetimes. Sometimes ancient memories rise to the surface, reminders that we are really divine fragments who will someday return to the Source. Life is both a dream and not a dream, Edward. Above all it is something to be lived rather than figured out. A celebration. Be at peace. All is well. It has always been so.

Immersed in the light, Edward lost track of time. It seemed that they were dancing together, he and Eldon, running across fields of flowers with colors brighter than any he had ever seen. …When Edward tired and stopped, Eldon kept running until he reached the crest of the hill. Another figure appeared just as Eldon arrived; a tall young man wearing a familiar green flannel shirt. They both smiled and waved. A hand on Edward's shoulder broke the spell.

"He be gone, honey."

It was Mary Blanchard.

Edward opened his eyes and looked at the body on the bed. The hand was cool, bony, the eyes open, sightless.

"Gone on," said Mary. "In the sweet bye and bye. Mrs. Muggeridge be gone, too. Sudden…"

"That's what she said," said Edward.

"What who said?"

"Mrs. Muggeridge. When I saw her this afternoon. Those exact words. I'll see you in the sweet bye and bye."

Mary leaned over and looked at Eldon.

"My, my," she said. "Mistuh Eldon here done look like he be smilin' when he leave us. Maybe he caught sight of Jesus."

She laughed that rich African laugh.

"This the first one you carried home?" she said.

"…Carried home?"

"First one you been with when they died…"

"Yeah," said Edward. "First one. We were running across fields of flowers, Mary. Huge blossoms with colors I've never seen."

"That'd be right," she said, nodding. "He loved his flowers."

"And Tommy was there."

"Your boy?"

"Tommy was there at the top of the hill. They waved and then disappeared. Both of them…gone."

"And you tried to follow?"

"I did," he said. "I did try to follow. But I couldn't."

"Not your time yet, honey…But it's nice when they let you come with 'em aways. You know, down the path. You has to be a good listener…gotta be empty so they can fill you. You know what I mean?"

"I think so," said Edward. "Maybe a little. God, what a day."

I'm exhausted, said Sarah. Why don't you go home so we

can both rest. I still get nervous when one of my students takes the first big step.

Why?

Because I want it to be a good experience. The earth is in dire need of people who are willing to be of service. In need of Teachers and Healers and Revealers.

And that's where I come in? said Edward.

Of course.

You know, I always wanted to be a Teacher.

Yes, said Sarah.

But there were these. . .difficulties.

Problems. . .a small matter of a police record. I understand.

And after that I wasn't such a great candidate for teaching.

True, said Sarah. But now, Edward, the good news is that you are actually in the process of becoming a Level One Teacher, a dispenser, if you will, of peace and of healing. The population of lonely frightened people is increasing far more rapidly than we ever imagined and we're very short of Teachers and Healers.

. . .So what do I do now?

Go home. Rest. Know that Tommy is well. Get up in the morning, do your morning meditation, ask the Great Pumpkin or the Force or even God for direction and go about your business assuming you've received it. Pay attention to the odd thought or hunch that comes your way. Watch for the signs. They may come in books, in conversations with small children, on billboards—they're everywhere. Someone may blurt out something that sounds really dumb. Listen, especially to that. Suit up and show up. That's the key. The Buddhists know— Attend! Attend!. . . Now you know—Row, row, row, your boat. . .It's very simple. Spread the message. Suit up and show up so you can Be There When It Happens.

. . .When what happens?

Ah, how I love your stout and inquisitive heart. But for now, Good night, sweet Edward. What is it Horatio says to Hamlet as he dies?. "May flights of angels bear thee to thy rest."...That right?

I think so, said Edward.

I have watched you for a long time, said Sarah. Long before you knew of my existence. All is well. It has always been so. And always will be. Go now and see how many faces of God you can find in the time you have remaining.

Sarah, I need to know more about what I'm supposed to do...

There was no answer. Outside the window, small brown finches clustered around the feeder, vying for a slender perch to stand and eat.

He got to his feet slowly. Mary put a stout arm around him and steered him out of the room. Tony joined them in the hallway.

"These folks be Home now," said Mary. "Eldon and Mrs. Muggeridge. They be Home now. Tommy, too. Runnin' in the light. No use frettin' over them. You go home and get some rest. Have some hot chocolate..."

"Relax," said Tony. "Go stand in front of the mirror and say applesauce. Yell it if you want to."

Edward stopped and looked at Tony, then at Mary.

"...You knew all along?" he said. "Both of you? About Sarah and...everything?"

They burst into laughter at the same time. In a few seconds he found himself joining in as they walked arm in arm down the hallway in the House of the Dying. In the background he thought he could hear the faint rustle of wings, but he couldn't be sure...Perhaps it was just the wind.

ABOUT THE AUTHOR

Edward Bear is a pseudonym. The author was born in Brooklyn, New York and grew up in Los Angeles, California. Early adventures included a brief stint in minor league baseball, too many years in construction, day labor and other dead-end jobs. Attended six colleges, received no degrees. A correspondence course in engineering landed him a job at Hewlett Packard where he was employed for nearly thirty years. Previous publications: several fiction pieces in small literary magazines and journals; a baseball novel, *DIAMONDS ARE TRUMPS*, St. Luke's Press (1990), *THE DARK NIGHT OF RECOVERY, Conversations from the Bottom of the Bottle*, Health Communications, Inc. (1999); and *THE SEVEN DEADLY NEEDS*, Health Communications, Inc. (2000). The elusive Mr. Bear currently lives high in the Rocky Mountains with his wife, plays a vintage Martin guitar and writes in whatever time the gods and goddesses have left him.

To contact the author—www.edwardbear.net
or
edbear01@aol.com

ORDER FORM

Please send____copies of *THE COCKTAIL CART* @ $12.95 plus shipping to:

Name:_____

Street:_____

City:_____

State:_____Zip:_____

Colorado residents add 7.3% sales tax (95 cents per book).

____Books at $12.95..$_____
Shipping...$_____
Tax (if Colorado resident)...............................$_____
                                        Total.......$_____

Shipping:
First Class: $3.50 for the first book and 75 cents for each additional book.

Send check or money order to:
M&J Publishing
P.O Box 460516
Denver, CO 80246-0516

(Make checks payable to M&J Publishing.)

If you do not have the money to purchase the book, just send in the order form and the book will be mailed to you without charge.

ORDER FORM

Please send____copies of *THE COCKTAIL CART* @ $12.95 plus shipping to:

Name:_____

Street:_____

City:_____

State:_____Zip:_____

Colorado residents add 7.3% sales tax (95 cents per book).

____Books at $12.95..$_____
Shipping..$_____
Tax (if Colorado resident)...............................$_____
                               Total.......$_____

Shipping:
First Class: $3.50 for the first book and 75 cents for each additional book.

Send check or money order to:
M&J Publishing
P.O Box 460516
Denver, CO 80246-0516

(Make checks payable to M&J Publishing.)

If you do not have the money to purchase the book, just send in the order form and the book will be mailed to you without charge.